To
Charlotte

FIRESEEDS

OF
SPIRITUAL
AWAKENING

Revised Edition

Dan Hayes

Campus Crusade for Christ International
Orlando, FL

Published by
Campus Crusade for Christ
Integrated Resources
100 Lake Hart Drive
Orlando, FL 32832
1-800-729-4351

Integrated Resources Product No. 1501e

Library of Congress Catalog Card 83-073130
ISBN 1-57902-030-5 (Previously 0-86605-130-9)

Printed in the United States of America

Unless otherwise indicated, scripture quotations are from the *New American Standard Bible*, © The Lockman Foundation 1960, 1962, 1963, 1968, 1971, 1972, 1973, 1975, and are used by permission.

Contents

Preface

Dr. Charles Malik, one of the founding architects of the United Nations, asserted in a speech at Wheaton College that "once [a person] realizes that Jesus Christ will find Himself less at home on the campuses of the great universities of Europe and America than almost anywhere else, he will be profoundly disturbed, and he will inquire what can be done to recapture the great universities for Jesus Christ, the universities which would not have come into being in the first place without Him."[1]

That is what this book is about: recapturing colleges and universities—not through political action, but through campus spiritual awakening. There is available to Christian collegians more joy, more power, more challenge, and more significance than they have ever imagined.

God is beginning to draw a spiritual force of students from all corners of our land which will, by God's grace, obliterate the massive apathy, purposelessness, and spiritual malaise that has afflicted our nation for years.

Spiritual awakening can come to our colleges and universities, and it may come soon. This book is written to help us get "on board," to get caught in the joyous jet stream of God's spirit as He sweeps across and through the campuses of America and the world.

In these pages can be found the motivation, perspective, methods, and results of massive spiritual stirrings in our residence halls, fraternities, sororities, athletic teams, and classes.

My prayer is that we might be stirred, motivated, and instructed to lay the foundations for spiritual revolution in the halls of academia. If we expect it, follow the principles outlined here, and not quit, we will see it happen.

It has happened before, and God can bring it in an even more sweeping way again. May we not miss the chance to cooperate with Him in helping university communities know personally the very Incarnation of Truth Himself, Jesus Christ.

Acknowledgments

John Donne said, "No man is an island." Certainly that is true when it comes to writing a book. No man writes one by himself. Therefore, I would like to offer my sincere thanks to some who have helped in the endeavor.

Roger Randall and the Campus Crusade for Christ national campus team helped me discern the needs of college students and offered many helpful suggestions.

Ney Bailey spurred me on when the going got rough.

Judy Steward spent many hours working on the original manuscript.

Claude E. Robertson, Jr., has helped me by organizing, editing, and typing the revised edition.

Thousands of college and university students have testified personally in the last ten years to the validity of the truths contained in this book and have, by their frequent critiques and insights, made many improvements in this edition.

My wife Charlotte and children—Janie, Danny, and Cindy—have exhibited the sort of love and patience that was necessary to allow this book to be written.

Without all of these men and women (and many more who played larger roles than I probably realized), this book and the benefits it has produced would have never been possible.

1

Let's Turn The College Campus Right Side Up

A record two out of every five freshman participated in an organized demonstration last year . . . . This figure continued a pattern of renewed participation in protests and other forms of activism, which is more than double the levels recorded in the late 1960's.[1]

The number of freshman college students in America claiming to be born-again Christians is probably the largest in the last 50 years. But though general student activism recently has increased, Christian students seem to have become less and less active and more passive in the last few years. It is ironic that believers on our campuses seem less concerned about the pressing moral and social issues of our time than those who make little claim to be Christians at all. We, who ought to be the salt of the earth and the light of the world, have instead become the vanilla extract and the bushel baskets.

As I move from campus to campus, I look for revolutionary Christians who will stand up and say they

1

are committed to living for Christ, no matter what the cost and no matter what they might have to sacrifice. But it is hard to find such Christians. With a large number now claiming to be born-again Christians (3.5 million out of a total student population of 11.5 million), we could be great agents for change if we want to.

Being an agent for change does not mean your college experience should be miserable. College is and should be fun. Nowhere else can you make the kind of friends that you make in college. Nowhere else can you reach new academic horizons like you can in the universities. Nowhere else can you have dates like the ones you will have in college (maybe). Nowhere else can you be trained for employment like you will be trained in college. Nowhere else can you get the feeling of freedom you get in college. Nowhere else can you have the joy of self discovery that you have in college. But all of this does not conflict with Christian students being genuinely revolutionary.

Sexuality and the Christian

The title of one of my most popular lectures on university campuses is, "Sex and the Search for Intimacy." My thesis is that the sexual revolution that began in the 1960's has been both a resounding success and a tragic failure. Part of my presentation encourages the audience to avoid self-destructive consequences of sexual involvement outside marriage.

Student after student will come up to me and say, "You know, Dan, you are right. After hearing what you had to say tonight, I have decided to stop sleeping around." The interesting thing about this is not only are non-Christians making these comments, but also believers are as well. Everyone—from the unbelieving community to the believing community—seems to be confused and searching for good answers about sex today. Everyone seems to be in the same unhappy fog.

Goals Without Purpose

Lack of purpose is also rampant. If you ask average students what their purpose in life is, they will say it is to get a degree and then get a job, buy a house, and have a big family. If you ask what their purpose will be after this, they often add a bigger job, a bigger house, a bigger family, and perhaps a bigger mate. Beyond that, they have no purpose. Yet these are actually no purposes at all. They are goals. Ultimate meaning seems to elude our universities and our society in general.

In The Great Midwestern Thinkoff, sponsored by the New York Mills Cultural Center, essayists seek to establish whether there is any purpose in life. Founder John Davis makes the following observation: "I think we have really struck a nerve with this. We supposedly live in this great information age, but nobody thinks any more. Nobody is challenged."[2]

And because they are not challenged to think, it is not surprising that most people have no overarching sense of purpose to govern whatever goals they have. They bounce from objective to objective and event to event, with no anchor to steady their paths. Students of today are just like everyone else: drifting, hoping to find purpose and meaning by landing the right job or finding the right family—only to discover that landing the right position or spouse is simply the springboard to finding yet another job and perhaps another spouse.

3

A fraternity president at a major American university who made straight "A's," was involved in student government, and was one of the most popular students on his campus told me he would lock himself in his room when the day was over and stare at the walls for hours because he had no purpose or direction in life.

Not only are students today lost in a sexual morass and a purposeless environment, but also the Christian position is mocked and disregarded on campuses across America. One of the problems of the "political correctness" movement is that it urges tolerance for any group or belief except those who would claim any sort of absolute truth, like Christians or other members of many of the world's great religions.

In the preface, I quote Charles Malik's observation that Jesus Christ is less welcome in the halls of our universities than almost anywhere else today. For example, battles go to the Supreme Court to determine whether it is even permissible for Christians to meet on campuses to pray. Christian students are excluded from jobs in residence halls because their Christian convictions do not allow them to acknowledge that all lifestyles are equally valid. Christian professors are intimidated by fellow professors for openly espousing a Christian, Biblical, or even moral viewpoint. Some are denied tenure and fired. Others must file lawsuits to be reinstated.

This has forced many Christian professors into being "closet believers," holding a personal faith but afraid to acknowledge it. At the same time, those who espouse a militantly anti-Christian view are forcefully dispensing it to all they teach.

Full Out or Fallout?

You may say, "But wait, Dan, I'm part of a Christian group on campus. I am an activist. I'm involved." If you are part of a group, that is great. But look around you. Would you describe your group as being revolutionary Christians who are "full on and full out" for Jesus Christ? Or would it be more accurate to say you are part of a Christian group? It may even be the largest Christian club on campus—but still a club nonetheless.

But ask yourself these questions: "Is there revolutionary Christianity on my campus?" "Is there an immense amount of spiritual power being released where I attend college?"

I Corinthians 4:20 has exploded like a bomb in my mental and spiritual life. It says, "For the kingdom of God does not consist in words but in power." In other words, being a Christian is not talking or writing "a good game" for Jesus Christ or knowing a great deal about Jesus Christ. The kingdom of God is described in terms of spiritual power. Is spiritual power being made manifest in seeing my prayers answered? Is there spiritual power manifested to introduce others to Christ? Is there spiritual power in my life to resist temptation and overcome evil? Is there spiritual power to move men for God and move God down to men through prayer? Is there spiritual power to disciple others in a way that is life changing for them and for me? Is there spiritual power to love my enemies, to pray for them, to do good for them, and to draw them to Christ?

The tragic answer on most of our campuses is that there is little revolutionary power and fire among Christians. There is little world-changing atmosphere. There is little desire to upset the *status quo*. Sadly, Christians more often are noted for what they do not do than for the power expressed in their lives. "I don't drink, smoke, or chew, and I don't go with those who do" is a saying which expresses how Christians are often perceived. Many are straddling the fence for Jesus Christ, with one foot in the world and one foot in the kingdom. One student volunteered, "I'm not sitting on the fence. I'm lying on top of it." But another countered, "He who straddles the fence is on the wrong side."

Making Him Boring

Sadly, Christians have done the one thing to Christianity and Christ that even Christ's enemies could not do. Christ's enemies scourged Him, mocked Him, beat Him, tried Him falsely, hung Him on a cross, jammed a crown of thorns on His head, stuck a spear in His side, and finally sealed Him in a stone-cold tomb. Centuries after His resurrection, His enemies denied that He ever existed. But with all this, we Christians have dealt Christ a more damaging blow. We have not killed Him, but we have made Him boring.

Instead of Christianity being perceived as the most exciting thing in the universe, we have portrayed it as lukewarm and dull. Instead of pointing to Christ and saying, "Hey, He is the greatest person ever!," we Christians have become just like many others in pursuit of the American dream, trying to baptize it with Christian clichés. Consequently, those who do not know Christ can legitimately ask the question, "Why would I want to become a Christian? There does not seem to be anything very different about them."

A further tragedy is that, while unbelievers remain skeptical about Christianity, Christians are not happy about this situation, either. Believers are not satisfied with being on the fence for Jesus Christ because they have in their hearts a desire to be totally involved for Him. A Christian life of mediocrity, selfishness, and fruitlessness only produces frustration and dissipation.

We have perhaps as many as 3.5 million Christian college students in America who have a desperate need for power, holiness, and New Testament vitality to characterize their lives. If their lives were changed, it would have a profound impact on the many who do not know Christ, no doubt bringing hundreds of thousands into the kingdom. We must ask, then, what is the solution? How can we meet this need?

The answer is revival and awakening on the American college campus. I believe God wants to move across all 3,200 of our campuses in sweeping power. I believe He wants to set the campuses aflame for Christ, to cause the believers to get off the fence and live enthusiastically for Him, and help to turn the entire system right side up for the kingdom of God.

Zeal Renewed

You may be thinking, "What is this thing called revival? I've heard about it, and it sounds like a pretty religious word. But it sounds pretty boring. What is it, anyway?" Charles Finney, a great clergyman of the last century who was responsible for helping much of America find revival, said, "Revival is nothing more than renewed zeal to obey God." It is renewed desire to be obedient to the God who made us and who always makes plans for our welfare. Individuals are changed and begin to move from selfishness to selflessness, from self-centeredness to love, from anger to patience, and from turmoil to inner peace. But while this happens all the time to individuals, I am going to use revival in a corporate sense. Revival also means a moving of God among great masses of people so that multitudes are turned very quickly to renewed zeal to obey Him.

J. I. Packer puts it this way:

> Revival I define as a work of God by His Spirit through His word, bringing the spiritually dead to living faith in Christ and renewing the inner life of Christians who have grown slack and sleepy. In revival, God makes all things new, giving new power . . . and new spiritual awareness to those whose hearts and consciences have been blind, hard, and cold.[3]

Such revivals are mentioned in Scripture, and there have been many in church history. This book will review some revivals that have happened on the college campuses of America to indicate how revival can occur again in this collegiate generation.

Starting in the early 1700's and moving through the 1800's into the early 1900's, there have been several movements of God's Spirit through the college campuses of America. The results of these movements were Christians renewed, self-destructiveness changed to wholeness, apathy to zeal, impotence to power, hate to love, indifference to passion, and carnality to spirituality. The result among unbelievers was equally startling. In some cases, one third to one half of the students of a university were affected, giving their hearts and lives publicly to Jesus Christ and going on to become fruitful disciples for Him.

8

The universities involved in such revivals are well known. Thousands were converted and discipled at such schools as Princeton, Yale, Harvard, Baylor, Emory, Cornell, Northwestern, and the Universities of North Carolina and Illinois. These later made a tremendous impact upon society for good and for God.

At Princeton University in 1875, a student Christian group known as the Philadelphia Society joined with the YMCA (which at that time was committed to evangelism and discipleship), with the following objectives:

1. The importance of seeking the salvation of students for their own sake and their influence as educated men.

2. The importance of securing their salvation while in college.

3. The value of united work and prayer.[4]

These objectives were to be achieved by the following:

1. Diligent study of the word of God.

2. Prayer.

3. Personal work (one-to-one evangelism).

4. Efficient organization.[5]

Through this effort, Dwight L. Moody was persuaded to conduct a series of evangelistic meetings on campus. As a result, nearly one third of the student body indicated they received Christ. Among those working with the Princeton YMCA were some of the most outstanding campus leaders of that generation. One such student evangelist eventually became president of Princeton University. Later still, he became better known as T. Woodrow Wilson, the twenty-eighth President of the United States.

Such experiences were common in American colleges and universities. Believers were stirred for God and thereby changed. Unbelievers were so stunned by these movings of God's Spirit and the difference in the lives of Christians that they came in droves to give their lives to Christ and to become part of great movements on their campuses. Christian society swelled, mission movements advanced, morality on campuses changed, professors were converted, great leaders came out of the movement, and major segments of the life of America as well as the life of the world were affected.

A Fifty-Year Wait

The last such massive movement on American campuses occurred 90 years ago. Virtually every campus in America was touched by that awakening. Perhaps as many as 10,000 to 15,000 missionaries went overseas from college campuses because of what God did in that awakening of 1905. Until that time, such collegiate awakenings occurred approximately every 40 years. But since 1905 there has been no nationwide American spiritual awakening. There have been a number of great evangelistic thrusts, but no sweeping revival. We are at least 50 years overdue!

Collegiate revival can occur in our day. In fact, you and I may well be the sparkplugs to help start the engine on the campuses that we influence. Dr. James Stewart of Scotland said:

> If we could but show the world that being a follower of Christ is no tame, humdrum, sheltered monotony but the most exciting experience the human spirit can know, then those who are standing outside the church looking askance at Christ would come crowding into our churches to

pay Him allegiance and we might well see the greatest revival since Pentecost.

Joining with hundreds of thousands of students on hundreds of campuses across America, we can have a part in seeing college campuses change and influence the history not only of the universities but also of our country for the next 100 years. Charles Finney said, "One way that we may know that revival is coming is when it is desperately needed."[6] It is desperately needed on college campuses today. I believe God wants to stir up our campuses again.

Turning Campuses Right Side Up

This book is intended to help you as a student or faculty or staff member become a sparkplug for spiritual revolution and revival on your campus. You are only one person. But by grabbing hold of the truth in this book, you can be used of God to influence thousands of your contemporaries for Jesus Christ. You can help turn the campuses of America right side up for the Savior.

Pause and ask God to make you available to be one of those people who will help spark a revival for God on your campus. You may have great natural abilities or not—this is not the issue. It is not your ability that God is looking for, but your availability. Before reading any further, tell the Lord that you desire to be available to Him to be used to help spark revival on your campus. Join with me and thousands of others who want to help shape the campuses of our country through revival. Do not be trapped by apathy or inactivity. Rather, seek to be involved in the greatest cause of all, that of Jesus Christ.

2

Awakened at Sixteen; Awakener at Twenty Six

> But though Josiah had these obstacles as a
> hindrance, there was one great obstacle which he
> did not have to overcome. He was not confirmed
> in sin. There is nothing so hardening to the heart,
> and so blinding to the eyes, and so searing to the
> conscience as sin. "Those who seek me early shall
> find me." Men who seek late in life, if they truly
> seek, will find, but it will not be such easy work for
> them as it is for the young.[1]

I have often heard the question, "Can we as university
students really do anything significant? We are young.
We do not have any resources. We are just studying and
working to get through school."

Yet students can be far more significant than we think.
Where God has been at work throughout history, He has
used young men and women to accomplish His tasks, to
further His purposes, and to interject into history those
awakenings that have changed its very course. Without
young men and women being available to God, many of

13

movements of history would never have

Let's look at the Word of God and at contemporary illustrations to see what God can do through people who are given to Him (young or not) and the means He uses. What are the criteria? What are the principles? What are the benefits? If we lay hold of these and understand them, then we can shake our campuses for God. Much of the skepticism and Christian apathy that now exists will be changed into heart-felt searching and finding of God and His Son, Jesus Christ.

The Worst of Times

II Chronicles 33 and 34 describe the worst and the best of times in Judah, Israel's southern kingdom. It has been ruled by a succession of good and evil kings. In Chapter 33 we see two of the worst of the worst: Manasseh and Amon.

Manasseh ruled for 55 years, and he had the distinction of being one of the most despicable kings who ever ruled any nation in the world. God said about him: "he did evil in the sight of the Lord according to the abominations of the nations . . . ." (II Chronicles 33:2) In other words, he was wicked like the kings of the heathen nations around him.

Not content with his own evil, Manasseh spent most of his free time involving everyone else in his sin.

> Thus Manasseh misled Judah and the inhabitants of Jerusalem to do more evil than the nations which the Lord destroyed before the sons of Israel. (II Chronicles 33:9)

One of the baser things that he did in Israel was to practice witchcraft and spiritism (II Chronicles 33:6). And he also encouraged people to sacrifice their children to the Gods of Molech and Baal on altars of fire.

When Manasseh died, his son Amon took over. He was much like his father, just less creative. II Chronicles 33:22 says, "He did evil in the sight of the Lord as Manasseh his father had done, and Amon sacrificed to all the carved images which his father Manasseh had made, and he served them." The only good thing you can say about Amon is that his rule was very brief. After two years, his own servants finally conspired to put him to death.

Josiah, the Boy King

Judah was now in a bad way. After 57 years filled with idolatry, witchcraft, murder, immorality, and all manner of heathen practices, the people had forgotten about God. They were materialistic. They wanted their own way, and they were uninterested in any sort of spiritual life. Yet sometimes the darker the night, the brighter the light. Into this scene enters the protagonist in this drama, Josiah the boy king. II Chronicles 34:1-3 tells us:

> Josiah was eight years old when he became king, and he reigned thirty one years in Jerusalem. And he did right in the sight of the LORD, and he walked in the ways of his father David and did not turn aside to the right or to the left. For in the eighth year of his reign when he was still a youth, he began to seek the God of his father David and in the twelfth year he began to purge Judah and Jerusalem of the high places, the Asherim, the carved images, and the molten images.

Josiah, the Praying Teenager

What a contrast to his grandfather and to his father. Only eight years old when he started to reign, Josiah evidently had within him a heart for God from the beginning. At age 16 he began to seek God fervently and earnestly. Evidently, this zealous quest brought him close to God. It grieved his righteous heart to see the practices of the palace around him and those of the nation that was named with God's own name. How many hours in the next four years must he have prayed and wept and thought and planned and strategized and studied until, gradually, ideas and directions came into focus. Even though still young, he knew what was necessary.

Josiah set out to eliminate idolatry from Judah and Jerusalem. He was like the sons of Issachar, who earlier "understood the times, with knowledge of what Israel should do." (I Chronicles 12:32) He never said, "I know things are really bad and what this society is doing certainly isn't glorifying God, but what can I do? Sure, I'm king. But I have all these older advisors around me, and they constantly caution me not to take any steps that would upset 'the applecart,' cause political upheaval in my kingdom, or stop people from paying taxes, or have them ask for a new king. I just don't think I'd better do anything very radical while I'm so young. I'll just wait until I become 50 or 60 years old. Then I'll be so respected that people will listen to me, and I can make all the changes I need to make."

Josiah had a very positive view of his own youth. He realized that he was in a position to help accomplish the total renewal and revival of his nation and society. He knew he had the energy. He had not been seared by habitual sin for years. He knew he was not tied down by as many responsibilities as he would later. As a young man, he was still idealistic. Though he had much to learn, he also knew he had a lot of time to learn it. He probably knew that he could also count on other men and women of his own age sharing his own convictions to follow him, forming an army that would accomplish Judah's cleansing.

Josiah ranged far afield from Jerusalem. In the cities of Manasseh, Ephraim, and Simeon (even as far as Naphtali and their surrounding ruins), he tore down altars, crushed carved images into powder, and chopped down all incense altars. Then he returned to Jerusalem.

This is a great story. This young man desired to destroy the very things that had brought dishonor to God ["They tore down the altars . . . " (II Chronicles 34:4)]. Josiah encouraged the people to return to God and confront the idolatry, apathy, and wickedness arrayed against them. In the face of opposition, he burned white hot with a passion for God and righteousness. This passion not only drove him, but also it caused many others to follow him.

In the space of about six years, all of Israel was outwardly cleansed of the idolatrous practices that had characterized the reigns of the two previous kings. Can you imagine? He turned the whole nation around in six short years—about as long as it takes some to finish college!

Despite Israel being outwardly cleansed of its unrighteousness, the deeper problem of inward cleansing and renewal remained. Though you can legislate, spirituality can only come from inside an individual and from inside a population. Josiah had made the right start and had accomplished more in a few short years than most people could in an entire lifetime. But how could the inward transformation of Israel be accomplished?

Josiah, the Righteous Young Man

While Josiah was probably pondering both the successes of his reign and what remained to be accomplished, a discovery was made during the cleaning and restoration of the temple of a lost book of the Law given to Moses by the Lord. Believed by most scholars to be the book of Deuteronomy, this restatement of the Law was intended to remind the people of Israel not to forsake their God and to warn what would happen if they did.

Josiah's response at this discovery was to tear his clothes. (II Chronicles 34:19) Whenever this is done in Scripture, it is a mark of great sorrow, grief, and repentance. This seems to occur when there is a renewed consciousness of the holiness, the majesty, and the presence of God Himself. It dawned upon Josiah that no one had read this book for 80 years, no one had believed it, and no one had followed it. Everyone had simply forgotten it.

"No wonder," Josiah perhaps thought, "we have experienced such immorality, violence, and unrighteousness in our kingdom. No wonder the people are so spiritually bankrupt. We have not obeyed God. In fact, we have not even known what obeying God means."

As a person who applied what he read, Josiah immediately took action. II Chronicles 34:29-33 describes what he did and the long-term response of the people to this new exposure to the Word of God.

Then the king sent and gathered all the elders of Judah and Jerusalem. And the king went up to the house of the Lord and all the men of Judah, the inhabitants of Jerusalem, the priests, the Levites, and all the people, from the greatest to the least; and he read in their hearing all the words of the book of the covenant which was found in the house of the Lord. Then the king stood in his place and made a covenant before the LORD, to walk after the LORD, and to keep His commandments and His testimonies and His statutes, with all his heart and with all his soul, to perform the words of the covenant written in this book. Moreover, he made all who were present in Jerusalem and Benjamin to stand with him. So the inhabitants of Jerusalem did according to the covenant of God, the God of their fathers. And Josiah removed all the abominations from all the lands belonging to the sons of Israel, and made all who were present in Israel to serve the LORD their God. Throughout his lifetime they did not turn from following the LORD God of their fathers.

God had undertaken to solve the second part of Josiah's dilemma: how to produce the inward change that would connect with the outward cleansing that he had accomplished in Judah. And he did this by providing the power of His own Word, which cut like a scalpel through Josiah and his friends and the people at large.

Revival of a Lifetime

Scripture reports that the people did not turn from following the Lord God of their fathers during Josiah's lifetime. No longer did they merely follow Josiah, nor did they simply exhibit a rigorous, fearful adherence to his kingly position. The people now came under the conviction of God's Word and desired to serve Him from within.

The next chapter of II Chronicles tells us that the Passover was celebrated as it had not been celebrated in centuries. In fact, this was probably the greatest Passover in Israel's history. This was not a legalistic response to Josiah, but it reflected a genuine refreshing that the nation had experienced on both an individual and on a corporate level. Awakening by God's Spirit had come!

It is incredible what God did through this very young leader of 26. What was different about Josiah? An examination of the record reveals four basic principles which allowed him to influence revival.

Only God Can Bring Revival

Josiah was effective because he knew that being king alone would make no difference—it was only God who could produce a spiritual awakening in his apostate nation. He knew he had to pray. When the Scripture says that Josiah "began to seek God at age sixteen," it means that he largely devoted himself to prayer.

"Yes," you say, "but can prayer really make a difference in non-biblical times?" The story of Samuel Mills illustrates that it can:

> As an entering freshman at Williams College [in 1806] Samuel Mills cut anything but an impressive figure. Mills was described by one of his roommates as having "an awkward figure and ungainly manner and an inelastic and croaking voice". . . .
>
> Soon after his arrival he came into contact with a group of fellow Christians who were meeting in

prayer for revival among students of Williams College. Fearful of contempt and possible disruption from their peers, the group met in the countryside some distance from the college. Although he was but a freshman he was also twenty-three and because of his maturity and the depth and sincerity of his own religious life, Mills quickly became the leader of these students.

The group continued to meet on a twice-weekly basis throughout the summer. One hot, sultry August afternoon, the skies began to darken and the accompanying thundershowers and lightning persuaded them to return to the shelter of the college buildings. Before they could reach the campus, however, the clouds began to disperse and they were able to continue their meeting under the shelter of a nearby haystack. After some discussion, Mills invited the students to join with him in offering their lives in the cause of foreign missions, so as to reach the under-privileged peoples of the world. "We can do this if we will," he said, revealing a determination differing from the expected "we will do this if we can."[2]

The impact of the resultant revival was so great that, "not only Williams College, but also Yale, Amherst, Dartmouth, Princeton, to name a few, reported the conversion to God of a third to one half of their total student bodies, which in those days usually numbered between 100-250."[3]

As with Josiah, it was the prayers of Samuel Mills and his compatriots that sparked a great awakening at Williams College and in all of New England. In addition, it launched one of the greatest foreign missions thrusts in the history of the world. All because they were willing to pray.

Josiah, the Activist

Young Josiah also was effective in the awakening of his day because he took action concerning his convictions. II Chronicles 34:3 reports that he began to seek the God of his father David, and he began to purge Judah and Jerusalem of the carved and molten images on the high places. Josiah was an activist. He knew that he could not do everything, but he knew that he could do something. He also knew that by his example and leadership others might be motivated to be activists in their spheres of influence. No doubt it was lonely being out on the cutting edge. But as he began to watch others fall into step with him (and perhaps sometimes accomplish more), it made all the loneliness and hardship worth it.

Taking a stand and being an activist is not an easy thing to do, particularly when you may receive ridicule from students, professors, townspeople, and others. But it always pays.

Bruce, the Activist

I had a friend in college named Bruce. He and I had been Christians about the same length of time, for about a year. We both had an English professor who was renowned on the campus as a skeptic. His classes numbered 300 to 400 every semester, and he delighted in taking every opportunity he could to discredit the Bible and the gospel of Jesus Christ. Semester after semester, unknowing students would write down what he said as truth and find their Christian faith (if they had any at all) completely undermined. This professor was very intimidating, and he would make a point of ridiculing anyone who would stand for his faith. Consequently, my approach was, "I'm just going to keep quiet and try and suffer through this class and hope I don't get ridiculed."

Bruce took a different tack. He decided he was going to take action and not allow his beliefs to be trampled without a struggle. One afternoon he approached this professor and questioned him about his statement about two allegedly contradictory sets of Ten Commandments in the Old Testament. Grudgingly, the professor pulled out a Bible from his shelf, blew the dust off, and opened it to show my friend "the error of his ways." After pausing for few minutes to search for the two passages, he looked up with a surprised expression and said: "Well, what do you know. There are two sets of Ten Commandments in Scripture, and they don't contradict each other after all."

As far as I know, the professor never taught that falsehood again. Bruce was willing to stand up for his faith and be an activist, even when his grade might have been in jeopardy. This experience emboldened him and me to become more aggressive witnesses for Christ.

The people who have changed the world have not necessarily been the smartest, nor the richest, nor the most powerful in terms of political structures. Instead, they have been those who have been willing to be activists for their faith.

Honest About Sin

Josiah was a man of prayer as well as an activist. In addition, he was honest about his own sins and the sins of his people. Not only did Josiah personally repent and tear his clothes when he realized his sin of ignoring the law, but also he was aware that, by the people's

23

trampling of the law of God, there was a dire expectation of judgment upon them. (II Chronicles 34:19, 21) His response was to confess his sin and the sins of his people and then expose his people to the Word of God so that they might personally repent, confess, and receive God's cleansing. This cleansing affected both individuals and the nation.

One passage on cleansing in the New Testament is I John 1:9: "If we confess our sins, He is faithful and righteous to forgive us our sins and to cleanse us from all unrighteousness." Confession means agreeing with God that our sins are wrong, they are forgiven, and they are to be turned from.

Josiah did not try to hide his sin. He did not try to blame others or belittle them. Rather, he acknowledged his errors and asked the Lord to cleanse him. This is the action we must take if we are to experience God's power in our lives and be avenues of God for spiritual awakening and revival.

The Student Preacher

Less than 80 years ago, there was another young man who was not afraid to call his compatriots to confession and repentance. He was Evan Roberts of Wales. Roberts, a student at Newcastle Emlyn College, had a profound experience with God. He experienced cleansing and awakening in his own life. With the permission of his college principal, Roberts left his studies and went home to the village of Loughor to preach his first sermon. His first message was heard by 17 people and consisted of only four points: confess any known sin to God and put right any wrong done to man, put away any doubtful habit, obey the Holy Spirit promptly, and confess faith in Christ openly. No one could have imagined the response.

Dr. J. Edwin Orr reported that within three months a hundred thousand converts had been added to the churches of Wales. Alcoholism dropped by 50%. Crime plummeted so much that some judges were presented with white gloves, meaning there were no crimes to try. There was even a work slowdown in the coal mines because so many workers became converted and ceased using profane language that the donkeys pulling the coal carts could not understand their instructions and had to be retrained with clean language.[4]

Roberts was not afraid to call sin by its name, ask for cleansing and forgiveness, and encourage others to do the same. The Spirit of God took the simple words of this godly young man, turned a whole nation right side up for righteousness and began a spiritual awakening that circled the globe within the next five years. It is estimated that millions came to Christ worldwide.

Josiah, the Summoner of People

Josiah was also not afraid to call other people to join him to pursue common ends.

> The king went up to the house of the LORD, and all the men of Judah, the inhabitants of Jerusalem, the priests, the Levites, and all the people, from the greatest to the least; and he read in their hearing all the words of the book of the covenant which was found in the house of the LORD. (II Chronicles 34:30)

Josiah was not simply giving them information. He was reading to them so that they might yield their lives to

God. He was calling them to become part of a great army for righteousness, a force that would be an army of love, holiness, and support to those who wanted to live for God. He alone could not do the work he had been given. It was necessary that tens, hundreds, and thousands of others be involved in a life of walking with the Lord and being a witness to the nations around him.

We can do that. In fact, we have to do that. None of us is strong enough, spiritual enough, talented enough, or smart enough on our own to be the only channel of blessing for our campuses or our communities. But each of us can call other people to be on our team. And as other people join with us, they can call still others to be a part. By a few calling a few (who in turn call a few more), a great movement can be built very quickly. Such a movement can permeate every segment of our campuses. It can also become a channel of spiritual power which can, in the providence of the Holy Spirit, touch the inner lives of students in ways we never could by our words, our persuasiveness, or our personalities.

At Berry College (a private secular college in Rome, Georgia), an awakening occurred in the mid 1980's because two students summoned others. With little organized Christian activity on campus, these two men became concerned about the welfare of their classmates. After reading this book, they decided to call others to join with them in their efforts at revival.

By their own testimonies, nearly 10% of the student body were in small-group Bible studies within two years, and Christian meetings had quadrupled in size.

Think of it! This happened because two students decided to pray and call others to be involved.

Here's the point—spiritual awakening frequently starts with men and women willing to go on a limb for Jesus Christ, to pray fervently for spiritual awakening, to live and be activists for the biblical convictions they have, to be honest in confessing their own sins and the sins of the campus or community in which they live, and to be unafraid to expose others to that same Word and Spirit from which conviction comes. Then they call others to the same challenge and task with which they themselves have been burdened.

Think back on Evan Roberts. He was only 26, he did not have a college degree, his first sermon was heard by only 17 people, he had not finished his college degree, and he was not an accomplished preacher. Yet he was willing to pray, to be an activist, to call others to come with him, and be honest about their sins. God used him and the others he reached to bring 100,000 people to the kingdom of Christ and change the moral climate of his country. Speaking at the 1994 Spring graduation at Colby College in Maine, former President George Bush said that if he had one wish, it would be "to restore America's inner moral compass." Evan Roberts' example gives us hope that we can play a part in restoring that compass for the campus.

Paul said to Timothy, "Let no one look down on your youthfulness." (I Timothy 4:12a) As students, we can see God use us in perhaps as great or even greater magnitude as Evan Roberts. But that is up to God. Let us never hide behind our own youth or inexperience to sell ourselves short. The time for spiritual awakening is now, and we can be the ones who will ignite it.

3

Five Prerequisites to Revival

> Many of you have already found out, and others
> will find out in the course of their lives, that truth
> eludes us if we do not concentrate with total
> attention on its pursuit.[1]

As we consider revival and awakening on our campuses,
the question we must ask is, "What is my part in seeing
revival and awakening come, and what is God's part?"
In seeking an answer, there are two things to keep in
mind. First, God Himself is the only source of revival.
He brings it, He establishes it, He conserves it. The
second thing to remember is that God often waits in
bringing revival until we have exercised our own faith
and obedience. We cannot do His part, but we can do
our part. Dr. G. Campbell Morgan once said: "We cannot
organize revival, but we can set our sails to catch the
wind from heaven when God chooses to blow upon His
people once again."[2]

As we study revivals, we discover five prerequisites that
help "set our sails" toward the wind of revival. If we

meet these, perhaps God will be pleased to bring spiritual explosions to these campuses of our country and those around the world.

Though these prerequisites are found throughout Scripture, they are especially encapsulated in what is the summary text on spiritual awakening—II Chronicles 7:13-14:

> If I shut up the heavens so there is no rain, or if I command the locusts to devour the land, or if I send pestilence among my people, and my people who are called by my name humble themselves and pray, and seek my face and turn from their wicked ways, then I will hear from heaven, will forgive their sin, and will heal their land.

The foundational requisites for revival in this passage are the following:

1. God's people must recognize that there is a desperate need for spiritual awakening.
2. God's people must humble themselves before him.
3. God's people must confess their sin and repent.
4. God's people must continually and earnestly pray.
5. God's people must call others to join with them to meet these prerequisites.

Let's look in depth at the first of these prerequisites.

God's People Must Recognize the Need For Spiritual Awakening

The context of II Chronicles 7:13-14 is remarkable. These are words given by God to Solomon at the apex of Israel's history. In essence, Israel was already in a time of spiritual awakening. The temple had been completed. Within it, the very presence of God, the *shekinah* glory, had come to dwell in the Holy of Holies. Solomon was revered throughout much of the world for his wisdom, and God received great glory because of it. There was no obvious spiritual declension in the land. Why, then, does God speak so "negatively" about pestilence, locusts, and drought?

He speaks of these because He knows that human beings do not do well in prosperity, whether spiritual or material. As John Wesley pointed out: spiritual prosperity brings diligence, diligence brings economic abundance, economic abundance produces laziness and greed, laziness and greed produce spiritual decline, and spiritual decline brings about God's judgment, necessitating another awakening.

What God seems to be saying to Israel is that it will be necessary once again to get their attention about their spiritual condition. Verse 13 tells us three ways (out of the many possible ones) He will do it: through drought, disease, and locust infestation. These manifestations are renderings, amazingly enough, of His grace. He is trying to help His people meet the first prerequisite for revival, recognizing the desperate need for spiritual awakening. And often the only things that get our attention are those things which cause us pain. "Pain," C.S. Lewis said, "is God's megaphone."

Though God may first send prophets, preachers, and his word to warn us, quite frequently it takes disaster and tragedy to strike hard enough to make us turn to Him for answers. This need recognition must come first in our list of priorities, or we, as God's people, will go on our own oblivious ways down paths to ever-greater harm.

If you polled a thousand Christian students on campus today regarding the moral apathy, spiritual breakdown, lack of purpose, and struggle with sin and asked, "Do you think we need an awakening today?," most no doubt would answer, "Of course, we do." But such nonchalant assent is not what I am talking about here.

Admitting something and being absolutely gripped to do anything about it are two different things. As Crawford Loritts has said, "'Is-ness' and 'ought-ness' are two very different things." Someone addicted to nicotine might know (in his head) that he needs to quit smoking. But he might only do something about it when lung disease finally strikes.

When a few Christians on a campus are gripped with the urgency to shake their college or university, they recognize the need for revival. They are not content to wring their hands in pious concern. They want to become personally involved in doing something to help bring revival to their campus.

What would be some analogous realities to the plagues and hardships of II Chronicles 7:13 in our society? Consider the following:

1. Extensive drug and alcohol use and epidemic addictions to them.

2. AIDS and other sexually-transmitted diseases (herpes, chlamydia, gonorrhea, etc.)

3. Sexual perversions considered normal and right.

4. The inability to build significant relationships (most vividly seen in dating and marriage).

5. Convenience killing of unborn children.

6. The rampant pursuit of power.

7. The unbridled pursuit of possessions.

8. The pursuit of pleasure as the focus of life.

9. The violence in our streets and in our neighborhoods—murder, robbery, rape.

10. The plague of pornography (including child pornography).

11. Child abuse.

12. Spouse abuse.

13. Racism (personal and institutional).

14. The elimination of God and religion as an issue to be discussed in our public educational system.

15. The overt hatred of God and Christ by some in positions of power.

16. The hearts of many fathers and mothers turned against their children, and the hearts of many children turned from their fathers and mothers.

If these are too cerebral and antiseptic to drive us to him, note the following news accounts:

Man Charged With Burning Two Sons to Death at Foundry

A man stopped by the foundry where he worked on his way to Thanksgiving dinner and killed his two young sons (two years and nine months old) by putting them in a large ladle and heating it.[3]

33

Commuter Massacre, Our Warning

The Long Island Railroad massacre has temporarily shaken America. That it took a shower of bullets in a suburban railroad car to outrage us, though, is a measure of our *complacency* about crime and violence in society . . . . Our first task is to recognize that it is foolish, and futile, to rely primarily on politicians to solve moral, cultural, and spiritual afflictions.[4] [Italics added]

Body of Missing Dancer Found

Suzanne Hill's burned body was found in a Northwest Portland trash bin, and the medical examiner confirms she died a violent death.[5]

Top TV Creators Shun Religion, Study Shows

Top Hollywood creators of the entertainment fare on television are predominantly secular in outlook . . . and shun religion, a new study finds.

It also finds that they seek to reform society towards their views.[6]

Son Held in Mother's Slaying

The 32-year-old man was arrested after a standoff with police. His mother was found shot and burned to death.[7]

"X" Marks The Spot (Sore Spot, That Is)

You can't blame America's generation X . . . for whining so much.

Their reality bites: broken families, fewer job opportunities, diminished expectations. Have you surveyed the pop culture landscape lately? You'd probably be whining, too.

While baby boomers had wholesome Dorothy Hammill, the busters have tough Tonya Harding. While boomers had the Smothers Brothers, X-ers have the Menendez Brothers. And while boomers played that gentle early video game Pong, busters relax with Mortal Kombat.

Wait, there's more:

The baby boomers had	*The baby busters have:*
Lassie	Snoop Doggy Dog
Talk of a Beattles reunion	Talk of New Edition reunion
James Dean	Luke Perry
Mrs. Robinson by Simon and Garfunkle	*Mrs. Robinson* by Lemonheads
Drive-in theaters	Drive-by shootings
The Brady Bunch	The Brady Bill
The Supremes	Salt-N-Pepa
Somebody to Love by Jefferson Airplane	*Somebody to Shove* by Soul Asylum
Tom and Jerry	Beavis & Butt-Head
Mood Rings	Nipple Rings
Dr. Marcus Welby	Dr. Dre
Woodstock	Lollapalooza
Gloria Steinem	Lorena Bobbitt
The Graduate	*Reality Bites*[8]

Supreme Court Lets Schools Go To Devil

Way back in 1962, the Supreme Court played God, writing its own commandments and expelling prayer from the nation's schools. It's been Hell ever since.

Who or what do you think rushed in when God was kicked out? Why do you think drugs, sex, and guns became entrenched in schools?

We can't write this spiritual rot off as afflicting only poor urban schools. Violence and drugs are trapping students in comfortable suburbs.[9]

None of the above are from tabloids. They are all part of our daily reality. How many more plagues, famines, and droughts do we need to grip us?

And gripped we must be because no revival ever comes unless at least a few Christians become inflamed with the need to see such an awakening. Josiah, Samuel Mills, and Evan Roberts were all overwhelmed with the need for change and turnaround in their situations. This is the first step, the first prerequisite to revival. If a person really sees the need for revival, then he or she will be motivated to do something about it. Those who say they see the need but never do anything about it are clearly signaling that they are not gripped with its urgency.

In John 2:13-22 we find the story of Jesus' cleansing of the temple. Upon seeing people selling animals and changing money in the temple, Jesus made a scourge of cords, drove them out of the temple, poured out their money, overturned their tables, and then said: "Take these things away; stop making my Father's house a house of merchandise."

Jesus saw a need to stop the defamation of the temple. He did not do as we often do. He did not wring His hands and say, "Oh, this is a terrible situation. What a mess we have here in this temple. Someone should clean it up. But that's not my job. I'm too busy doing other good things like miracles. And, after all, I certainly wouldn't want to offend anyone by being too strong in my point of view."

Jesus not only saw the need, but also he did something about it. The editorial comment that John makes after this event sums it up: "His disciples remembered that it was written, 'Zeal for Thy house will consume me.'" (John 2:17) The King James version says, "Zeal for thine house hath eaten me up." Jesus was "eaten up" with the need to do something about the problem. What consumes the Christians on my campus? What grips us? The tragedy is that most of us are gripped or consumed with very little other than our own comfort, preservation, and plans for the weekend.

Have you realized that the need on your campus is so great that, apart from God manifesting Himself in grace and power, no appreciable change can occur? Have you and your Christian friends felt the burden for awakening in such a way that you will take action? Is there anything that grips you so strongly that, if God does not do it, you will become physically sick? As management expert Bobb Biehl asks, "What makes you weep and pound the table?"

The zeal and fervency which the Lord Himself can and must produce in us are needed so that we will be willing to pay whatever price is necessary to bring revival and awakening to our campus.

Two examples demonstrate both the recognition of a need for revival and an appropriate response.

In the Fall of 1984, I spoke at a large weekend conference for university students in California. More than 500 attended, representing over 30 colleges and universities.

Many of these campuses (some even without any full-time Campus Crusade for Christ staff) had 20, 30, and even 100 students in attendance.

But UCLA, the location of the very first ministry of Campus Crusade for Christ and a very important link in the university system of California, had only eight students attending—all men. This number was pretty dismal for a student body of over 30,000. Many other campuses with much smaller enrollments had more conferees than this large school.

Some of the UCLA students came and asked what I thought could be done differently. They had tried many things in their program to get students committed. More students would come to their meetings, but these eight were their only committed students.

I asked if they had yet come to the point where they realized that the only real hope for both their campus and the Crusade movement was to see God sovereignly and supernaturally stir them up in spiritual awakening. Each one of them replied that they had: they had reached the end of their and Campus Crusade's resources.

I then suggested that they begin to meet the other criteria for spiritual renewal and not quit until God had really blessed them in a significant way. In a time of prayer together, they admitted their need and admitted that they had not been fervent in laying the foundation for spiritual awakening. They also asked for God's enablement in the days to come.

Shortly after speaking at this conference, our third child was born. In the midst of the adjustment this brought in the next eight months, I periodically thought of UCLA but gave them very little focused attention in either my prayers or my thinking.

The next summer I was teaching a course in Campus Crusade's Institute of Biblical Studies, and one of the students in that class was from UCLA. In talking with him one day, he asked me the following question: "Well, I guess it is pretty interesting what happened at our school, isn't it?" Since I had heard nothing, I asked him to tell me more.

The story which he told me was remarkable because it was apparent that God had intervened.

After such low commitment prior to the Fall conference, they began to take very seriously the admonition to meet God's criteria. So those eight men began to meet daily to pray for revival and decided that, no matter how long it took, they were not going to quit.

Within a period of a few weeks, not only did the meeting size begin to grow, but also students began to talk spontaneously about their own lack of commitment to Christ and their desire to change. This produced very fertile ground for the next conference on the agenda, the California Christmas Conference. After taking only eight students to the Fall Conference, the movement now took 45 to the Christmas conference (more than a five-fold increase!).

Upon their return to campus for the Winter quarter, individuals began to pray each week in larger numbers in a group they called "Hour of Power," a prayer time strictly for revival on campus. Students crowded to get involved in discipleship and evangelism. The average weekly meeting now numbered 175. And when an Intervarsity traveling evangelist came to the campus in February, the Campus Crusade for Christ students banded together and did one-on-one evangelism among the large crowds that he drew. Hundreds of students heard the gospel that week!

In the Spring quarter they decided to have another weekend conference. Instead of eight students coming, over 100 attended this one; and hearts were changed in deep and powerful ways. When the Campus Crusade staff left for their summer project assignments, the entire ministry was turned over to students for the remainder of the quarter. This resulted in even greater commitment to the movement.

Eight months following the weekend Fall conference, the Campus Crusade movement sent over 40 students to Summer projects. While they were unable to get more than eight students to come to a weekend conference in the Fall, they were able to send five times that number to serve Jesus Christ for six to eight weeks the next summer. Truly, some sort of awakening had started.

As I tracked the ministry at UCLA the next year, I discovered that God did still more in their prayer meetings and in the total movement. A giant outdoor prayer meeting involving all of the Christian groups on campus was so significant that the front page of the student newspaper, *The Daily Bruin,* carried a photograph and a large article about the work that God was doing on that campus. When I asked students what God had done to change things, their immediate response was to look at me in surprise and say, "Obviously, it was prayer and our willingness to meet God's criteria that allowed Him to work in such a great way on our campus."

(When I asked a Campus Crusade for Christ staff member some years later what had caused that awakening to dwindle after the third year, he ironically said, "No question about it. We began to overorganize God's work.")

What is important to note about what God did at UCLA is that it would never have occurred if the eight students had not met the first of God's prerequisites—that they be gripped with a need to do something about the spiritual condition of their movement and their campus.

Another example of recognizing and responding to the need for revival involved a friend of mine named Read Williamson, a Methodist minister. He attended Vanderbilt University with my wife and had pastored in Tennessee for a few years after graduating from seminary.

Shortly after his wife gave birth to their second child, Read was diagnosed with a malignant brain tumor that was spreading. After some months, he was hospitalized. Initially, he was very discouraged, not being able to minister and knowing that death was imminent. But soon he realized that there was at least one big thing he could do: he could pray.

My wife Charlotte visited him in the hospital, and they discussed the need for spiritual awakening. At his request, she gave him a large poster on the subject, which he placed on the wall opposite his bed so that he could see it. As he viewed that poster, his zeal to pray for the students of America was energized. He would often pray and speak with visitors about Christ and the need for spiritual awakening and for a great movement of God on the college campuses of America and the world.

Though Read fell into a coma for a few days before his death, his wife reported that he uttered recognizable words about her and the children from time to time. "Occasionally," she added, "you could recognize that he was praying. And he would often pray for spiritual awakening on college campuses of our land!"

Here was a man of God at death's door, ready to make the great transition form the land of the spiritually dying to the land of the totally alive. And those things on his mind and heart, those things which gripped him (even in unconsciousness) were his family and the college campuses of America.

After communicating Read's story to a group of students from Virginia, I received a letter from a leader at Virginia Tech. He said: "We very much enjoyed your story about Read. I have yet to read it to myself or in a group without crying. Wouldn't it be great if we could all have that kind of commitment to prayer and spiritual revival?"

In all likelihood, currently you are not at death's door. Most of us probably have many years left to serve Christ. If we could be gripped with the need for revival like the students at UCLA in the mid-1980's and like Read, God might be pleased to send awakening to our campus and to our entire country.

Before discussing the second prerequisites for revival and awakening, let me suggest three action points.

First, take a piece of paper and list at least 15 reasons why you believe your campus needs spiritual awakening. Keep it in a place where you will see it daily.

Second, make it your daily prayer that God would burden you and your friends with the need for spiritual awakening on your campus.

Third, talk to others about this need and hold each other accountable.

By doing these simple yet profound things, you are taking the first step towards spiritual awakening on your campus.

4

Humility and Its Role in Revival

Put in simple terms, humility means to live as close to the truth as possible: the truth about ourselves, the truth about others, the truth about the world in which we live. It has nothing whatever to do with a Caspar Milquetoast kind of personality. It does not mean groveling or finding the worst possible things to say about ourselves.[1]

An associate of mine was once going through a very difficult series of circumstances that seemed to have no end. A friend seeking to comfort her said, "Mary, surely all these experiences are making you really humble."

To this she replied, "I couldn't be humble. If I were really humble, I would be proud of it!"

One said he could write a book and title it, *Perfect Humility and How I Attained It.* Humility inspires a lot of humor, probably because most of us do not know what it is. Yet from a study of history and the Word of God, it is very clear that, without humility, revival cannot occur. Thus humility is the second prerequisite for spiritual awakening.

Humility is not thinking less of myself than I ought to think. Sometimes Christians believe that humility is saying, "I'm a worm. I'm only a worm. I cannot do anything. I will be a doormat to every person, place, and thing that wants to walk over me." Not so! Humility means valuing myself with the same value that God places upon me, namely that Christ was willing to die for me. The dignity of man is defined by the life of Jesus and the cross of Calvary. And if Jesus Christ was willing to do this for me, then I can do something significant for him.

In this vein Dr. Howard Hendricks, professor at Dallas Theological Seminary, tells the story of a student who came to him and said, "Professor, pray that I might be nothing."

Dr. Hendricks replied, "No, I won't pray that you'll be nothing. You take that by faith. What I will pray for is that you will believe God to use you because of how significant a person you are because of Christ's work on your behalf."

Another misconception about humility is that it is something some people have and some do not. But no one is naturally humble. Some may seem more humble than others. But that does not necessarily mean they are. Humility is not natural. It is a quality imparted by God, and it is possible for all of us who know Jesus Christ to see that particular quality become more and more a part of our lives.

One does not become humble by thinking a lot about it. Instead, humility manifests itself in individuals' lives as they focus on something or someone else. Rather than concentrating on the quality they are trying to develop, they forget about themselves as they concentrate upon the other person or thing.

Seeing Ourselves in Him

In the context of revival and spiritual awakening, humility means being occupied with God and seeing ourselves in relationship with Him. It means that we see ourselves as creatures, and we see Him as Creator. We see ourselves as unworthy before Him; but, when viewed through His eyes, we see ourselves as worthy in light of Christ's life, death, burial, and resurrection. By ourselves we are weak, but in Him we are strong. We see ourselves as unable, but we see ourselves able in Him. We see our inconsistencies, but we see them as spaces through which His grace can flow.

Having seen the need for spiritual awakening, we should then bow before the Lord individually and corporately and admit that we cannot make spiritual awakening happen. But He can. If anything is going to change we admit that He is the one who is going to change it. We admit that in ourselves we cannot ignite the fire. But as we ally ourselves with Him, He can ignite a great spiritual conflagration that will spread over the campuses of our nation and the world.

Humility means that we admit we are willing to have fellowship with, pray with, and work with other believers who might think differently. It means that, although all of our doctrines might not be in the same slots, we are willing to focus on the same ends, namely seeing our campus ablaze for God. Humility means that we are willing to do anything, go anywhere, and say anything in order to seize spiritual awakening. In every age and time, it has been this sort of humility that has ignited believers and allowed them to become channels of the Holy Spirit to draw thousands of Christians and non-Christians to the foot of the cross and out into the world to exalt the name of Christ.

Humbling ourselves before the Lord and its relationship to revival is clearly illustrated in Isaiah 57:15:

> For thus says the high and exalted One Who lives forever, whose Name is Holy, 'I dwell on a high and holy place, and also with the contrite and lowly of spirit in order to revive the spirit of the lowly and to revive the heart of the contrite.'

Note here that the Lord says He dwells in two places. First, He dwells in a high and holy place—He is lofty, He is exalted. He is Creator, and we are creature. We bow before Him because He alone is worthy of our trust, love, and homage.

The Muslims have a saying in Arabic, *"Allahu Akbar"*—"God is great!" This effectively communicates how we are to see God if we are to be humble before Him. We praise Him as majestic, as awesome, as great. He is separated from us by loftiness and grandeur.

God has a second dwelling place, however. According to this passage, He also dwells with the contrite (humble) and lowly of heart. He lives next to, with, and in those who are humble of heart. His presence and availability here are real to those who admit their need.

The moment we recognize Him as high, lofty, and holy and act accordingly by acknowledging our own creaturely status, weakness, and need, He transfers His dwelling place from transcendence to immanence. He is right next to us, in us, and with us, closer than any relative or friend. All of His mighty presence and power becomes our present possession when we yield ourselves to Him. He becomes our friend, our power, our strength, the resource to meet our every need.

The One whose heart burns for revival more than any other now becomes our daily resource to produce revival and awakening in our situation. To those who humble themselves, God promises "to revive the spirit of the lowly and to revive the heart . . . ."

What is the converse? It is that God does not revive the proud. We have usurped God's place if we and other Christians on campus say: "We've got it together. With a little more hard work, materials, staff workers, and money, we'll do the job." We could stay on our knees until they fuse to the floor, and we would never see revival because we are not humbling ourselves. God only brings awakening to those of us who say, "Lord, we can't, but You can."

Alcoholics Anonymous has popularized the saying, "you will either humble yourself or you will be humiliated." So it is on campus. If we refuse to take action, God may bring us greater difficulty for a greater fall. It is far better that we choose to take action now.

A comparison of the current state of Christian activity on our American campuses as compared with the time of the last nationwide awakening 90 years ago is quite humbling.

In the first decade of this century, the total population of this country was 60 million, and university students numbered less than one-half of one percent of the population. The YMCA, then essentially an evangelistic organization, listed 30,000 collegians on its roster (17.6% of all U.S. students).

The comparisons to today are startling. Out of our current population of about 250 million, seven million students (or three percent of the country's population) attend universities. And of this number, no more than 80,000 (or merely one percent of today's students) are involved in evangelistic organizations like Campus Crusade for Christ, Intervarsity Christian Fellowship, and the Navigators.

In 1993 Intervarsity's triennial missions conference at the University of Illinois drew approximately 18,000 college students. Campus Crusade for Christ's Christmas conferences around the country had an attendance of 8,000. This total of 26,000 was only less than one half of one percent of the nation's total residential campus population or one-sixth of the proportion of the YMCA conference in 1906.

If we were to equal the student involvement of the earlier part of this century, we now would have 1,232,000 students involved in our campus ministries. And if we used only the 200 U. S. campuses where Campus Crusade for Christ has a presence, this would mean an involvement of 7,500 students per campus. And if Campus Crusade expanded to 800 campuses, each would have 1,540 active students.

With 41 times more students in America today, we have been unable to increase by even three times the gross numbers in our largest interdenominational campus Christian organizations. Even more sobering is the fact that our proportional involvement relative to the total student residential population has decreased by 88% in this time.

Apart from God's supernatural and providential acts at much higher intensity that we are currently seeing, we will never equal or exceed the level of student involvement in evangelistic organizations of 90 years ago. We must humble ourselves and admit our vast inadequacy "to make it happen" purely on the basis of better methods, materials, and communication systems. We must cry out, "O God, we can't! But, O God, You can!"

This may seem very discouraging. You may even be tempted to give up before you begin. Sometimes this is the way I feel. A conversation with a friend from Wright State University in Ohio helped. As we were discussing some similar issues one day, he said, "The real issue in humility is not how far down you get but how far up you can go after you get down."

So it is here. The issue is how much more God can do now, not how much is still undone. We must individually and corporately be burdened for revival and see the need for spiritual awakening. Bow before the Lord and ask Him to move His dwelling place from the high and lofty place to us, His people.

Billy Graham, A Modern-Day Example

An example of the power and promise of humility is seen in the life of evangelist and Christian statesman Billy Graham. Here is a man who has spoken and preached to more people than any man who has ever lived. During

50 years of personal ministry, he has maintained godliness, holiness, and Christian standards of integrity, even in the face of attacks and defections by others. Though he has received many honors and had a number or opportunities for financial reward, he has consistently followed the calling of God to win men and women to Jesus Christ until the Lord Himself returns.

One incident in Billy Graham's life clearly illustrates the nature of humility and its results. In 1945 Billy was almost 30 years old, already a fairly well-known evangelist, and president of Northwestern College in Minneapolis. He had, however, no national recognition, nor did he seem destined for any. He was obscure in what was considered the fundamentalist subculture.

At this same time, an outstanding young Canadian evangelist named Charles Templeton was beginning to have serious doubts concerning the authenticity and reliability of the Scriptures. He went to graduate school to attempt to resolve his doubts, but they only grew more intense. He and Graham often discussed these concerns, and soon he subtly began to challenge Billy's commitment to the authority of Scripture and suggested that He should re-think his position on the Bible.

At a conference center named Forest Home in Southern California in 1949, Billy was deeply hurt to hear of a remark by Templeton implying that Graham's ministry would be curtailed and he would never do anything significant for God if he continued to believe, trust, and preach the authority of the Bible. In his definitive biography of Billy Graham, John Pollack describes this time of struggling before the Lord:

> After supper, instead of attending the evening service, he retired to his log cabin and read again

the Bible passages concerning its authority. He recalled someone saying that the prophets used such phrases as "the Word of God came to us" or "Thus saith the Lord" more than 2,000 times. He meditated on the attitude of Christ, who fulfilled the law and the prophets: He loved the Scriptures, quoted from them constantly and never once intimated that they might be wrong.

Billy went out in the forest and wandered up the mountain, praying as he walked, "Lord, what shall I do? What shall be the direction of my life?" He had reached what he believed to be a crisis.

He saw that intellect alone could not resolve the question of authority. He must go beyond intellect. He thought of the faith he used constantly in daily life: he did not know how a train, or a plane, or a car worked, but he rode them. He did not know why a brown cow could eat green grass and yield white milk, but he drank milk. Was it only in the things of the spirit that such faith was wrong?

Graham later described his own thoughts: "So I went back and I got my Bible and I went out in the moonlight. And I got to a stump and put the Bible on the stump, and I knelt down, and I said, 'Oh God: I cannot prove certain things, I cannot answer some of the questions Chuck Templeton is raising, some of the other people are raising, but I accept this book by faith as the Word of God.'"[2]

What had Graham done? In humble faith and with great risk, he had placed his doubts and questions in the hands of his Creator. He humbly admitted that he did not have every answer. But he could trust God for the answers that he did not have. What followed can only be attributed to the God who "revives the heart of the contrite."

Two months later, Billy Graham launched what was then an experimental evangelistic tent crusade in Los Angeles. It exceeded all expectations and hopes. So many thousands of people were converted and so many multitudes of Christians were revived that the crusade committee extended the campaign from three to eight weeks. Such attendance at a Christian meeting was unprecedented, as were the numbers of conversions. Many Hollywood personalities and even underworld figures were converted. Many gave public witness to the change in their lives.

The final service drew 9,000 people. This was by far the largest evangelistic crusade in America in over three decades!

He had been largely unknown to the American public prior to this time. Now *Time* and *Newsweek* both wrote about the "new" evangelist, Billy Graham. The Associated Press carried dispatches across the nation. Graham's ministry suddenly accelerated around the world. William Randolph Hearst, owner of a vast newspaper empire (which included the *Los Angeles Times*), issued his famous instructions to his reporters: "Puff Graham!" The work of God became something that the secular press would write about, a phenomenon that had not been true in America for years.

Why did this happen? It happened because one man, William Franklin Graham, Jr., was willing to humble himself before God at great risk of failure, to look foolish and be pitied by his more "learned" contemporaries. He yielded everything (including his doubts) to the Lord of the universe. He decided to let God fulfill His promises to "dwell with the humble and contrite of heart" and to "revive the spirit of the lowly and revive the heart of the contrite."

Of course, Billy Graham's ministry and stature has continued to grow, even though he is now in his mid-70's. In early 1994, he journeyed to North Korea and met with leader Kim Il Sung. The *Wall Street Journal* reported: "It is notable that Mr. Kim would use a man of God to convey a message to President Clinton . . . . Billy Graham has a way of touching the hearts of men and women everywhere."[3]

His life is an example of impact stemming from humility. Could a great impact be made on your campus? Can you and a small group of other believers yield your rights, your possessions, your future, and perhaps even your doubts and prostrate yourselves before the God of the universe? Take the risk. Tell Him that, though you are weak, He is strong. And while you are unable, He is able—able to produce a spiritual explosion on your campus that will start a movement that will last for decades.

To feel the need of God like this is wonderful. One does not need to have all the answers. In fact, it may be better to know you have fears, doubts, and questions. Joe Brown, senior pastor of Hickory Grove Baptist Church in Charlotte (North Carolina), said, "I don't find in the Bible where Jesus condemned people for asking too many questions. I do find where he condemned people for thinking they had all the answers."[4]

If you have questions and know you do not have all the answers, take a few minutes now to meditate on Isaiah 57:15 and consider its implications for you and your campus. Tell God that you are willing to lay everything before Him: your life, your future, your studies, your money, your ministry, your doubts and fears. Ask Him to fulfill His promise to revive you. Then begin to expect miracles to happen.

5

Confession and Repentance

> Our Fathers believed God was offended by sin.
> They themselves were deeply troubled, both by the
> existence of personal sin in their own lives and by
> the presence of unconfessed corporate sins in the
> churches and in the nation . . . . They sought the
> Lord in . . . connection with wars, murders, rapes,
> etc., believing such outbursts of wickedness to be
> directly related to the general decline of moral and
> spiritual life in the churches.[1]

The third prerequisite for revival is confession and
repentance. II Chronicles 7:13-14, the scriptural
cornerstone of revival, contains the caveat, "turn from
their wicked ways." This is the hinge upon which the
door of revival may open. Without this, it will not come.

Sin is the great curse of life. It was the downfall of Adam
and Eve. It meant the human race needed redemption
from the pit into which it had fallen. Sin necessitated
that the Sin Bearer Jesus Christ take our sins on Himself
in order that we might be restored to fellowship with
God.

Sin short circuits God's power. It blocks the flow. It renders Christians fruitless and impotent. It puts "an elephant on the air hose." It blocks God's good intentions for each of us and "steals, kills, and destroys." (John 10:10) The flow of revival and spiritual awakening on your campus is clogged by sin.

Sin takes many different forms. The more obvious outward acts include drunkenness, abuse of drugs, and cheating. One tragedy of our day is that many Christians who participate in these acts are not even aware they are sinning. These behaviors are self-destructive and block our fellowship with God.

Proverbs 7:6-23 describes those who have sexual intercourse outside marriage. Verses 22 and 23 describe the final result of this sin. It is not pleasant: "Suddenly he follows her, as an ox goes to the slaughter . . . until an arrow pierces through his liver, as a bird hastens to the snare, so he does not know that it will cost him his life."

The seriousness of such sin cannot be overemphasized. With tears of frustration, a third-year medical student at the University of Minnesota recently told of trying to tell two girls, 13 and 14, that they would never be able to have children because of a sexually-transmitted disease.

Sin may be fun for a season, but it is a short season. It eventually brings physical, emotional, and spiritual devastation. The tragedy is that Christians get involved in these things more and more deeply, thereby undercutting their fellowship with God and the genuine abundance of life that Christ has planned for them.

It is important to understand that sin runs more deeply than just the more obvious outward acts. Romans 3:23 states, "All have sinned and fall short of the glory of God." *All* refers not only to those who are flagrantly sinful, but also it refers to those of us who are much more subtle and socially acceptable.

Coldheartedness, lukewarmness, criticism, backbiting, prayerlessness, and caring more about the approval of others than the approval of God are just as sinful and sometimes more difficult to mend.

Such a list could go on and on. It includes compromise with evil in order to "make the grade," cheating, lying (even little "white" lies), unrestrained anger against a brother or sister in Christ, uncaring attitudes toward the lost, and general indifference to spiritual issues. The list could also include racism, hatred, envy, and various conscious-troubling issues. These all qualify as sin which short circuits God's mighty power in our lives and weakens us. But before God can bring revival and spiritual awakening, we who are burdened for it and are humbled before Him must first be cleansed and empowered.

Every revival includes confession and repentance from sin. In his account on the Hebrides Revival in Scotland, J. Oswald Sanders reports:

> Around 1950, there was a powerful movement of the Spirit in the Hebrides. The awakening did not just happen. For some months a number of men met three nights a week for prayer; they often spent hours. The weeks passed and nothing happened until one morning at about two o'clock. A young man read Psalms 24, verses 3 to 5, "Who may stand in his holy place? He who has clean hands and a

pure heart, who has not lifted up his soul to falsehood and has not sworn deceitfully. These shall receive a blessing from the Lord."

He closed the Bible and, looking at his companions on their knees before God, he cried: "Brethren, it is just so much humbug to be waiting thus night after night, month after month, if we ourselves are not right with God. I must ask myself, is my heart pure, are my hands clean," and at that moment something happened. God swept into that prayer group and at that wonderful moment seven Elders discovered what they evidently had not discovered before, that revival must be related to Holiness.... They found themselves in the searching power of the presence of God and discovered things about themselves they had never suspected. That the blood of Calvary heals and cleanses . . . . These men found themselves lifted to the realm of the supernatural. These men knew that revival had come.[2]

We must be clear about what confession and repentance entail. Proverbs 28:13 says: "He who conceals his transgressions will not prosper, but he who confesses and forsakes them will find compassion." This verse specifically warns that we should not cover our transgressions. Concealing them is hypocrisy and leads to disaster in our Christian lives. Be honest. God knows what we are really like. We do not have to "pull the wool" over anyone's eyes. To seek revival, we must be genuine.

Confession: Agree With God

After honesty comes confession. Basically, confession means to agree with or say the same thing as God. When we confess our sin, it means two things. First, it means I admit my sin is wrong. I take responsibility for it. As

Scott Peck says, "we cannot solve a problem by saying it's not 'my problem' . . . . I can solve a problem only when I say, 'This is my problem and it's up to me to solve it.'"[3]

Second, I need to agree with God that Christ died for that sin and that it was forgiven at the cross. He died for all my sins, even the ones I commit ten years from now. I agree that He has paid the price, and I accept this by faith.

Confession involves exercising faith in the promises of God. I John 1:9 tells us that "if we confess our sins, He is faithful and righteous to forgive us our sins and to cleanse us from all unrighteousness." That is a promise. To make it true in our experience, we must trust it, rely upon it, and have faith in it. Then it becomes operative in our lives.

Confession means that I bring each individual sin before God. I acknowledge it as wrong and thank Him that it is forgiven. I do not seek to hide it. Rather, I bring it into His light and the light of His word.

Let me give you an example. At the height of the student radical movement in 1970, an event occurred at Asbury College in Kentucky. This, though, was a radical spiritual awakening that showed the power of confession.

> It began when a few concerned students began to meet to pray for spiritual awakening. On February 3, Asbury students went to a normal 10 A.M. chapel service. As sometimes happened, the dean did not give a message but instead asked students to share testimonies.

> Those who came forward were unusually fervent in telling what God was doing in their lives. One

senior said, "I am not believing that I am standing here telling you what God has done for me. I have wasted my time in college up to now, but Christ has met me, and I am different. Last night the Holy Spirit flooded in and filled my life and now for the first time ever, I am excited about being a Christian." As the end of the chapel hour approached, the bell sounded for classes to begin, but went unheeded.

Students confessed sins such as cheating, stealing, bitterness and drug use. The editor of the school newspaper had skipped chapel, but when he heard what was going on he came and hid in the corner. Eventually the Holy Spirit touched him: "I knew things in my life were a lie . . . . I was a sick and miserably lonely young man. Yet I sat there for two hours refusing to do anything . . . . There came that critical moment when I was forced to admit that my self sufficiency was failing me and I needed to be dependent upon Jesus Christ. I prayed at the altar for an hour and a half undergoing a spiritual revitalization."[4]

Sometimes sins need to be confessed publicly (as in the case of the student newspaper editor). But sometimes sins are best confessed only to the Lord. As J. Edwin Orr says, the amount of public confession should be "just enough to enlist the prayers of people right with God. The public confession of secret private sins might be dangerous."[5] Public sins should be confessed publicly; private sins confessed privately.

Repentance: Change Your Thinking

We come now to the area of repentance. Repentance does not mean feeling sorry about your sin (as most people think). Recall Proverbs 28:13: "he who confesses and forsakes [his sin] . . . will find compassion." Indeed, godly sorrow for sin may produce repentance, but sorrow is not itself repentance. Repentance, the Greek word *metanoia,* means to change your thinking. Implied is a change of action, a change of direction. It involves forsaking sin. When one repents of his sin, he cannot go on consciously committing it without remorse.

Repentance brings results that affect what we do. Students stop getting drunk. Racial attitudes are changed. People live with greater compassion. Sexual immoralities cease. Members of the opposite sex treat each other with respect, not as objects to gratify their own urges. Cheating ends, theft stops, and backbiting and unjust criticism become things of the past. In other words, lives and situations dramatically change in times of genuine repentance.

Restitution: Repayment

After confession and repentance of sin, restitution sometimes needs to be made. Restitution simply means repayment. If I have sinned against someone by word or deed, I may need to ask for their forgiveness or make some sort of repayment for what I have done. This is one of the hardest corollaries of confession and repentance. For example, I need to tell my professor if I have cheated on a test. It may cost me a lot. It may cost me my place in college, or it may cost me a grade in that course—but it will not cost me nearly as much as refusing to make restitution. If I have stolen, I need to repay. If I have assassinated someone's character, I must make it right with that person.

Restitution is a very powerful concept. Dr. Stephen Olford illustrates its results:

During a time of spiritual awakening in Africa, we are told that the police authorities were astounded at the genuine repentance and restitution that was made not only by converts, but by backsliders who were restored to the Lord. *The Daily Dispatch* of East London, South Africa, listed the following articles returned by repentant believers: 80 sheets, 25 blankets, 24 jackets, 34 trousers, 11 overcoats, 6 women's coats, 25 dresses, 27 skirts, 50 shirts, 22 bedspreads, 64 hats, 23 towels, 1 table, 4 chairs, 50 pillow slips, 15 scissors, 5 hairclippers, 9 wallets, 4 cameras, 4 wristwatches, 3 revolvers and ammunition, 30 tumblers and an assortment of jewelry, tools, cigarette lighters, crockery, cutlery, boots, shoes, pressure stoves, frying pans, lanterns, and safety razors.[6]

After speaking at a conference, a young professional woman came up and asked if I could help her solve a problem. She had garnered many honors during her university years, and she had been the outstanding student in her field of study. She was an officer in her sorority and in many clubs. She had already made many friends among the faculty and the administration. Her grade point average was 4.0.

While taking an examination during the Spring quarter of her sophomore year, her professor snatched the test paper from her in the middle of the session and instructed her to meet him in his office afterwards. Startled, she complied.

At their meeting, he said to her: "Young woman, you know why you are here—you know you were cheating on that exam. You have two choices: you can take an automatic "F" in the course, or, because we have an honor code here, you can bring it before the honor council and appeal it. But I am sure you would not want to do that because we both know you were cheating."

Her response was one of outrage. She replied: "I most certainly will appeal. I was not cheating. I will take it before the honor council." She stalked from the room, called her parents and the president of the university to protest this miscarriage of justice, and began to gather character references.

When the hearing was held, the professor presented his case for her cheating, and she presented hers. She was exonerated and received an "A" in the course.

In her junior year she encountered Campus Crusade for Christ, became a Christian, and became very involved in the movement. After her senior year she graduated from that university as the outstanding student in her field and moved into her chosen profession.

Sadly, she continued: "The only problem with this story is that I really was cheating on that exam. I could not admit it because I knew what it would mean to my reputation, my academic standing, and my parents and friends. Even after I became a Christian and God began to speak to me about setting this right, I did not have the courage to do it."

I asked about the consequences she was experiencing as a result. She replied that, whenever she sought to advance spiritually, it was as if Satan had her on a leash. He would jerk that leash and say, "Yes. Great Christian. You are really a spiritual giant. You made a professor in his first major teaching job look stupid, and you did not have the courage to admit your guilt. How can you ever move forward?

She asked what I thought she should do. I repeated Dr. Orr's advice: public sin needed to be confessed publicly and private sin needed to be confessed privately. I asked her, "How public was it?"

She looked sheepishly and replied: "How public was it? The president of the university was involved. My parents were involved. Faculty members were involved. Everybody knew about it." Since her sin was very public, I suggested she needed to find those involved, confess, and make any restitution needed. She said: "How could I do that? I might lose my degree, my academic standing. It even might affect my career." I asked if she would rather have short-term pain now or long-term pain for the rest of her life.

She saw what I meant. I offered to pray for her, hold her accountable, and call her if she wished. I also asked her to let me know about the progress she was making on this.

Six to eight weeks later, I received a letter that included another letter. In her letter she described her efforts to get things "right" with those to whom she had lied at her university and how she had tracked down her former professor (who was now at another college). She also described how she had confessed to her parents and received their forgiveness. The second letter was the response from the wronged professor she had written.

In his letter, the professor responded with astonishment that she had contacted him after the intervening years and acknowledged that it had been difficult knowing that, despite her denial, she really had cheated. He then expressed his forgiveness to her. He added: "I am deeply impressed with your willingness to admit that you cheated on the exam. That single act shows a significant depth of character that most people lack. I know that you spent many sleepless nights and anguished over writing the letter before finally doing so. The fact that you wrote is an indication of your moral fiber and your conviction as a Christian. I will always be impressed that you contacted me after all these years. Good luck with your career and with your future. Both are extremely promising."

When I called to ask how she was doing now, she replied: "I'm free. I'm really free."

In the years since, I have seen her on several occasions. Both her career and her life have moved forward with great fruitfulness. The lessons are obvious. Even when there is great personal cost and risk, the process of confession, repentance, and restitution is worth it.

It is not easy. But if our campuses are to see spiritual awakening, we Christians must be cleansed. We cannot hold on to sin, short-circuiting God's mighty power. When we confess our sin and repent of it, we are cleansed vessels, available for the Holy Spirit to fill and use us. We are able to be powerful in our walk with Christ and in our witness. Our prayers will start to be answered in greater abundance and fruitfulness.

If we do not confess and repent, the Holy Spirit is grieved and quenched. No fire of God will fall upon our campus—at least none resulting from our efforts.

You who are burdened for your campus and for the work of God at your college or university need to come before God, confess the sins He lays on your heart and repent, make restitution when necessary, and be available to be filled with God's mighty power by faith. Calvary precedes Pentecost. It we want the Spirit to manifest himself in great glory, the "crucifixion" that is repentance and restitution must come first.

Here is an exercise that has worked for thousands of students. Take a sheet of paper, a pencil, and your Bible. Ask the Holy Spirit to show you any areas that are displeasing Him. Take 30 minutes to an hour and make a list of those sins.

Then tell the Lord you acknowledge them as sin and accept by faith His forgiveness. (I John 1:9) Determine by His power to turn from them and expect the Holy Spirit to fill you with His power. Make restitution or public confession where necessary. (It may be tough, but it will be worth it.) If you were sincere when you did this, you will be a cleansed vessel ready to become a glowing spark of revival and awakening on your campus. You will be ready to be involved in the fourth prerequisite of spiritual awakening—praying fervently that such a revival will come.

6

The Supreme Example of Prayer

The great people of the earth today are the people who pray. I do not mean those who talk about prayer, nor those who say they believe in prayer; but I mean those people who take time and pray. These are the people today who are doing the most for God; in winning souls; in solving problems; in awakening churches; in keeping the old earth sweet awhile longer.[1]

Some may ask: "If Jesus and the Father are always at work in the world (John 5:17), why do we need some special work, a revival, anyway?" Arthur Wallis tells this interesting story from nature:

There was once an ancient reservoir in the hills that supplied a village community with water. It was fed by a mountain stream and the overflow from the reservoir continued down the stream bed to the valley below. There is nothing remarkable about this stream. It flowed on its quiet way without even disturbing the boulders that lay in its path or the foot bridges that crossed it at various points. It seldom overflowed its steep bank or gave the villagers any trouble. One day, however, some large cracks appeared in one of the walls of the old reservoir and soon afterwards the wall collapsed and the waters burst forth down the hillside. They rooted up great trees; they carried along boulders like playthings; they destroyed houses and bridges and all that lay in their path. The stream bed could not now contain the volume of water which therefore flowed over the countryside, even inundating distant dwellings. What had before been ignored or taken for granted, now became an object of awe and wonder and fear. From far and near, people who in the usual way never went near the stream hastened to see this great sight.[2]

Like the gentle stream, God is always at work. But when He comes in exceptional power, this like a raging torrent, this is revival. Nothing is the same. People who have never thought about God now think of no one else, talk of no one else, and concentrate on no one else.

God desires to manifest Himself in power. He wants to come like this raging torrent to overturn the things that stand in His way on the campuses of America today. We as Christians have a tremendous opportunity to help prepare the way for such a movement.

Confession and repentance (including any needed restitution) are vital to prepare us to lay hold of God. But we also need something else to lay the foundation for revival. II Chronicles 7:14 says, "if my people . . . will pray . . . ."

Prayer for revival (not Grandma's bunions or Cousin Herman's toothache—but for genuine spiritual awakening) is the channel through which flows God's revival power. We must pour out our hearts in a fresh

70

way for the salvation of our family and friends, for our campus, for the morals of our country. This stimulates our faith and demonstrates to God that we are serious about our requests. He then answers those prayers by bringing a fresh spiritual awakening.

No vast spiritual movement has ever occurred without being preceded by fervent prayer by groups of believers. If you count the 2,000 years of Christianity as just such a movement, we find they also were immediately preceded by three and one-half years of fervent prayer by Jesus Christ.

A study of Jesus' personal prayer life started a radical change in my prayer habits. It added new power to my life and ministry. It also launched my burden for awakening. An examination of several aspects of Christ's prayer life hopefully will motivate us to move forward in our praying so that we can see God's mighty work on our campus for His glory.

Although Jesus was fully God, He was also fully human. As a man, He depended upon God the Father to meet His every need and to accomplish His entire ministry. There is much evidence in Scripture that His prayers were the very channel through which God's power flowed into Him, enabling Him to do mighty exploits.

In Luke 11 we see the disciples after one year of following Him and observing His ministry. They want similar results in their own lives and ministries and ask Jesus to teach them how to receive them.

Interestingly, they did not ask about the mechanics of His miracles. Rather, they came to Him with the request, "Lord, teach us to pray."

These twelve men had begun to realize the secret of the power and ministry of Jesus' life—the intimate prayer time he spent with His Father. They also realized that the only way that they were going to experience similar results was to learn how to tap into God through prayer.

Jesus was a master teacher of prayer—not just through His words, but through His life. As we survey His ministry, we see the tremendous importance of prayer in much of what He said and did. This should motivate us to lay hold of God so that our lives and ministry can take on the characteristics of the divine.

Beginning in Prayer

We read in Luke 3:21, "Now it came about when all the people were baptized, that Jesus was also baptized, and while He was praying, heaven was opened."

It is significant to note that Jesus was praying at the very outset of His ministry. While He was praying, heaven itself was opened and (as we read later) the Holy Spirit descended upon Him and God the Father spoke audibly. Jesus knew that, before the launching of any great enterprise, it was vital to spend time with the Father, talking to Him about future events and asking for His power and love to accomplish the task set before Him.

The founding of Campus Crusade for Christ is an example of a successful enterprise being launched with fervent prayer. Initially, founders Bill and Vonette Bright saw only mediocre results from their evangelistic work on the UCLA campus.

Then in 1951 a 24-hour prayer chain was started in many churches of Los Angeles for UCLA. The day was divided into 96 different 15-minute periods, with people praying around the clock.   ✳ Why not now?

Following the inauguration of this prayer movement, the very first evangelistic meeting at a sorority house was held, and over half the women present indicated they wanted to know Jesus Christ personally. In evangelistic meetings with various fraternities, sororities, and athletic teams which followed, there were similar responses. And hundreds of students that year found salvation in Jesus Christ.

By the end of that first year at UCLA, over 250 students were newly converted, including many of the most outstanding student leaders on the campus. Such were the changes that even the campus chimes, which had previously played secular music, now began to play hymns at noontime!

Continuing in Prayer

Jesus Christ began His ministry in prayer, and He persevered in prayer throughout His earthly life. An important verse is Luke 5:16: "But He Himself would often slip away to the wilderness and pray." This refers to his habit of prayer. Prayer was not a haphazard activity of our Lord. He engaged in prayer as the norm of His life. One might ask, "When did He pray? In what situations was prayer called for?" J. Oswald Sanders gives us an overview:

> He prayed in the morning at the gateway of the day (Mark 1:35). He prayed in the evening when the day's work was over (Mark 6:46).

Great crises were preceded by prayer. It was while he was praying at His baptism that heaven was opened. This was the watershed of His life and ministry, for He was identifying Himself with the Godly remnant of the apostate nation.

He prayed in the hour of His popularity, the time when so many are swept off their feet. His selection of the twelve apostles, a seemingly unimportant yet in reality epic-making event in world history, was made only after a night of prayer (Luke 6:12- 13). It was after a special time of prayer that he opened His heart to his disciples and shared with them the dread fact of his approaching suffering and death (Luke 19:9-28).

It was while he was in the act of prayer that the majestic transfiguration scene was enacted and the approving and authenticating voice of His Father was heard (Luke 9:29, 35). Prayer was the cause, transfiguration was the effect. Is there a lesson here for us?

✳ Great achievements were preceded by prayer. Many miracles followed prayer: the feeding of the four thousand, the feeding of the five thousand, walking on water, the raising of Lazarus, and the healing of the insane boy. Each of these miracles was linked with the prayer that preceded it.

✳ Great achievements were followed by prayer. When confronted with great crisis, we turn instinctively to prayer, but once the crisis is over, the task achieved, we tend to lean on our own abilities or wisdom. Jesus guarded against this evil by following such occasions with prayer.

Great pressure of work was a call to prayer. Our Lord's life was exceptionally busy. He worked under constant pressure. At times He had no leisure even for meals. But whatever the pressure, He made sure that prayer did not become a casualty. To Him, it was a call to devote extra time to prayer.[3]

In short, Jesus prayed all the time. There was never a time when He did not pray to meet the tasks, the pressures, the burdens, and the joys of His day. Prayer was the consuming passion of His life.

Ending in Prayer

He began in prayer and continued in prayer. He also ended His ministry in prayer. On the night of His betrayal and capture, He fortified Himself (as Luke 22 informs us) by going to the Garden of Gethsemane, falling on His knees, and spending an extended time of prayer with His Father. He warned the disciples, "Pray that you may not enter into temptation." He knew the reality of those words. Prayer was the antidote to temptation and sin. He knew that the temptation to do His own will could be counteracted only by extended time with the Father. In similar circumstances, we might find ourselves anxious and concerned. But Jesus concentrated upon His Father and demonstrated His need to depend upon Him at the end of His ministry.

And even Jesus' final words on the cross were a prayer: "Jesus, crying out with a loud voice, said, 'Father, into Thy hands I commit my spirit.' Having said this, He breathed His last." (Luke 23:46)

How could He end His life in such a powerful and prayerful way? Because the practice of Jesus' life was prayer, it was also the way He chose to end it.

Praying Today

What is Jesus doing today? Hebrews 7:25 tells us: "Hence also He is able to save forever those who draw near to God through Him, since He always lives to make intercession for them."

Jesus Christ is continually interceding for us in heaven today. He has not stopped. The habit of His earthbound life is the habit of His heavenly life. We are always on His mind, and He is always presenting us before the Father in His prayers.

S. D. Gordon comments: "The Lord Jesus is still praying. Thirty years of living; thirty years of serving; one tremendous act of dying; nineteen hundred years of prayer. What an emphasis on prayer!"

He began in prayer, He continued in prayer, He ended His ministry in prayer, and He continues in prayer today. What an example to us of the importance of prayer!

If we are to see awakening and see our campuses change for good and for God, we must learn to follow the example of our Savior and become men and women of prayer. As a starter, begin to set aside at least 15 minutes a day for personal prayer, talking to God about the needs on your campus. It may be difficult to persist this long in the beginning. But as you persevere, you will soon find that 15 minutes is not too long. Then find someone else to pray with you. This joint prayer time could be the small beginning of a massive awakening.

Challenge !

7

The Power of Fervent Prayer

> Through prayer, God has given us the privilege of
> being used by Him to help change the lives of men
> and nations. God has made available to us a vast
> reservoir of power, wisdom, and grace beyond
> words to define, if only we are willing to believe
> Him and claim His promises.[1]

Prayer has always been the precursor to revival. If we
commit ourselves to prayer, there is no limit to what we
can see God do. Genesis 32:26 gives us Jacob's
instructive prayer to God: "I will not let you go unless
you bless me." (Genesis 32:26) This is the kind of
fervency and persistence that needs to characterize our
prayers. He is saying, "You can't make it rough enough
for me to stop. I am holding on until you fulfill your
promises."

This is very difficult for us to do. William Raspberry says
we are "the nation that lives for short term gain.
America is addicted to the short term."[2] In prayer, that
is doubly true. We pray a while. When no obvious
positive answers are forthcoming, we become distracted
or discouraged and quit. But lasting revival is brought

by continual prayer for a spiritual brushfire to break forth on our campuses, convert the lost, quicken the Christians, and focus the campus on Christ Himself.

The Prayer of One Person

Consider the example of one man. James 5:17 tells us, "Elijah was a man with a nature like ours, and he prayed earnestly that it might not rain; and it did not rain on the earth for three years and six months."

Elijah was a weak and sinful man, but he loved his great and powerful God. He prayed that it would not rain so that evil King Ahab would be brought to his knees before God.

God heard Elijah's prayer, and He answered specifically. For three and one-half years there was no rain. People turned to God, and Ahab finally admitted his need for a divine solution.

Elijah prayed again. This time, he prayed it would begin to rain. And it poured. Like James later commented, "The effective prayer of a righteous man can accomplish much." (James 5:16)

Do you believe this? If so, start consistently praying for revival on your campus. If you learn persistence in doing this, much will be accomplished.

Consider another illustration of what one person's praying can accomplish:

> In a certain town there had been no revival for many years; the church was nearly extinct. The youth were all unconverted, and desolation reigned unbroken. There lived in a retired part of the town an aged man of so stammering a tongue that it was

painful to hear him speak. On one Friday, as he was at work in his shop, alone, his mind became greatly exercised about the state of the church and of the impenitent.

His agony became so great that he was induced to lay by his work, lock the shop door and spend the afternoon in prayer.

He prevailed and on the Sabbath called on the minister and desired him to appoint a conference meeting. After some hesitation the minister consented, observing however that he feared that few would attend. When evening came, more assembled than could be accommodated in the house. All were silent for a time, until one sinner broke out in tears, and said, if anyone could pray, kindly would he pray for him? Another followed, and another, and so on, until it was found that persons from every quarter of the town were under deep conviction. And what was remarkable was that they all dated their conviction at the hour that the old man was praying in his shop. A powerful revival followed. Thus this old stammering man prevailed and as a prince had power with God.[3]

We are not talking about the need to be a spiritual giant. Rather, we are talking about ordinary people with a giant God who make an extraordinary effort to pray for awakening.

Multiplying the Prayers of a Few

If one person praying for revival is good, two or more are better. Jonathan Edwards, one of the premier human channels of America's First Great Awakening, said, "When God has something very great to accomplish for His church, it is His will that there should precede it the extraordinary prayers of His people."

A few college and post-college men met for prayer in Philadelphia in 1857 and 1858. They became burdened for revival and launched a daily prayer meeting in November 1857. At first, only a few attended; but they were not discouraged. They continued. Soon the room contained 20, then 30, 40, 50, and finally 60. The fervency of prayer increased. One could sense an explosion about to occur.

Four months after they began to pray, the revival began:

> At first, only the small room was occupied, with a few in attendance. Then it became overflowing, and the meeting moved to the main saloon, meetings starting there on the tenth of March. Twenty-five hundred seats were provided, and were filled to overflowing. The sponsors next removed a partition from the main floor space and platform; next, the floor platform and lower gallery, then floor platform and both galleries filled up; fully six thousand people gathered daily.

> For months on end each separate church was opened at least each evening. Some of them as often as three and five times a day and all were filled. Simple prayer, confession, exhortation and singing was all that happened, but it was so honest, so solemn, the silence so awful, the singing so overpowering, the meetings were unforgettable.

> In order to continue the work, which flooded churches with inquirers and converts, a big canvas tent was bought for $2,000 and opened for religious services on May 1, 1858. During the following four months, an aggregate of 150,000 attended the ministry under the canvas, many conversions resulting. The churches in Philadelphia reported 5,000 converts thus won.[4]

These numbers are even more amazing when you consider that the total population of Philadelphia at this time was less than a tenth of its current size. Affected by the same revival and awakening, the adjacent state of New Jersey recorded over 60,000 converts within a few weeks. At the same time, 40% of the students at Princeton were converted and 18% entered full-time Christian ministry.

This awakening was a part of the revival known as "The Laymen's Prayer Awakening." Perry Miller, the great Harvard historian, chronicles the total number of converts to Christ (and added to the churches) in America between 1858 and 1860 as one million, or 3.2% of the U.S. population. (An analogous number of converts today would be eight million.) Dr. Miller called this revival, "the event of the century."[5]

The pray-ers were unknown individuals. Few have found their way into history books. They were just ordinary folks. Yet through their prayers, they were responsible for thousands of converts and for multitudes of believers being set on fire for God. These percentages and numbers may seem mind boggling in light of the spiritual apathy we often note among many of our classmates. But if we take our minds off of the numbers and place them on the pray-ers for revival and their fervency in prayer, then something similar can happen among us right now.

The people who prayed in Philadelphia caught the "prayer spirit" of their Master. Similarly, we can be infected like that today. Indeed, this infection is already spreading across our country and around the world.

Praying for Revival Today

In the last ten years, I have received hundreds of letters from students all over the country detailing their burden for prayer and revival. And they have been putting their concern into action. Early in the morning and late at night and at noontime students on multitudes of campuses are praying for revival at their schools. One would be hard pressed to visit a major residential campus today and not find a group (or many groups) of these fervent pray-ers.

The following are only the tip of the iceberg:

[Stanford University:] "It was very rare twenty years ago to find vital, vibrant religion on the college campus," says David Rosenhan, a professor of law and psychology. "Now there are prayer meetings that are attended by 300-500 students regularly."[6]

[The University of Illinois:] "A groundswell of religious ardor is creating a breadth and depth of religious participation that has not been seen in American colleges in decades. At least 9,000 of the 35,000 students are active members of religious organizations. There is a spiritual dimension in the lives of these young people I did not notice ten years ago," declares the fundamentalist Jerry Falwell.[7]

[Brown University:] We praise You for the fervency you have given us and ask You to increase it. Start a fire burning. There is nothing we desire more than for God to sweep across the campus.[8]

[Harvard:] I have become completely convinced that we will never find in ourselves or our fellowships the kind of passionate, powerful spirit of prayer spoken of by all those greats gone before until we, like they, make seeking this life of prayer the first commitment of our life and ministry. Because it is first, it does not come by seeking it second. That is why, for me, my covenant of prayer . . . has become absolutely essential in helping me to enter into a life of continual, fervent, believing prayer, which I am completely helpless to achieve, but can only receive by the Holy Spirit.[9]

[High Schools:] Take heart, though! Nearly 1200 high school students from 30 states and some youth workers converged together at the Hyatt Regency Hotel in Minneapolis for "Something's Happening USA '91." They met over Labor Day weekend. For three days, these young men and women gathered to pray and to seek God. They were challenged to be intimate with God, to be holy, and to walk in purity and righteousness. It was a challenging and convicting time. They were exposed to the need for spiritual awakening in America and specifically on their campuses.[10]

[Duke University:] As a student . . . I had the opportunity to watch a body of believers take to their knees and then see the Lord work. There had been a few prayer warriors and some very significant things happened as a result of their obedience. But when the whole body was united in vision and in prayer, a power was unleashed that we had never known before. Individual lives were changed, Christ was made an issue on campus, the gospel was proclaimed, and Duke University was witnessing a revival it had not seen in nearly a hundred years.[11]

[Auburn University:] During our regular 7 A. M. Monday morning prayer, the students organized a "Jericho Walk" around the Coliseum. We walked around seven times (just like the Israelites), praying for different things . . . . We prayed for 3,000-4,000 people to attend [a Josh McDowell meeting] . . . . The Coliseum personnel assured us we would not have more than 1200 total. We know a God who is a big God, so we prayed big! What a thrill it was to watch people begin to file into the Coliseum at 8 P. M. . . . As 8:30 came (the time the lecture started), we looked up at all the faces and saw 3500 people! It was fantastic . . . . God really blessed the evening.[12]

[Churches:] For over two years, I have trained and coordinated cooperative prayer movements . . . On every hand I have been confronted with an interest in prayer—even a sense of divine timeliness for it. [It] tells me the hour is right for a sweeping prayer movement . . . . Nothing else seems quite as critical right now.[13]

The most dramatic Christian revival today is in the country of South Korea. The church there is growing at a rate of 6.6% per year, mostly through conversions. It is projected that by the year 2000, 42% of South Korea will be Christian. This is amazing because only 10% was considered Christian in 1971. Thus the population of this primarily Buddhist country of 30 million will have had its Christian population grow from three million to 12 million people in 29 years![14]

How did this happen? There are many factors, but the probable genesis of this movement reaches back many decades. J. Oswald Sanders relates the following:

Some years ago a great revival swept over Korea, the fruits of which revival remain to the present day. This revival had been prayed down. Four missionaries of different denominations had agreed to meet together to pray daily at noon. At the end of one month a brother proposed that "as nothing had happened," the prayer meeting should be discontinued. "Let us each pray at home as we find it convenient," said he. The others, however, protested that they ought rather to spend more time in prayer each day, so they continued their daily prayer meetings for four months. Then suddenly the blessing began to began to be poured out.

In less than two months more than two thousand heathen were converted. In one church it was announced that a daily prayer meeting would be held every morning at four-thirty. The very first day four hundred people arrived long before the stated hour, eager to pray. The number rapidly increased to six hundred. Heathen people came to see what was happening. They exclaimed in astonishment, "The living God is among you!"[15]

Commenting on this, Dr. Joon Gon Kim, respected Korean pastor and Campus Crusade for Christ East Asian Director, says:

In 1907 at Pyongyang seven hundred people were dramatically filled with the Holy Spirit while attending a week-long Bible study conference. This conference is often referred to as the Korean Pentecost. The lives of those attending were changed. They began their new lives as fireseeds of prayer, founding a nationwide prayer movement which continues today. The fireseeds became witnesses for Christ, used mightily to start spiritual fires across our nation and into many corners of the world. Fireseeds traveled to China, Japan, and America. Anywhere Korean people assembled a spark seemed to ignite.[16]

More recently, Bill Bright wrote the following:

In Korea . . . we have helped to train over two million Christians who have gone from Korea to the ends of the earth with burning hearts. There is no place in the world where one finds a greater emphasis on prayer and fasting. God has honored that spirit, and today the influence of Dr. Kim and the Korean people embrace the world . . . . Their zeal for Christ, their personal prayer life, their revival spirit prompts them wherever they go throughout the world to have a vital impact for the Savior.[17]

The Korean revival began in prayer, it continued in prayer, and it goes on now at an accelerated pace. Tomorrow morning at 4 A.M., millions of South Koreans will rise, dress, and go to homes and churches to pray for the reunification and Christianization of Korea.

How can you catch their enthusiasm for prayer? You can do three things.

First, make a list of all the biblical promises on prayer, especially those relating to revival. II Chronicles 7:13-14 would be a good place to start.

Second, pray daily for revival on your campus and in your dormitory or Greek house. Ask God for greater fervency and a spirit of persistence. After all, this is the basic meaning of I Thessalonians 5:17: "Pray without ceasing."

Third, join with others who are praying for revival. Decide to meet regularly to pray.

The following passage has pricked my prayer life for years, and I hope it will be equally stimulating to you:

> The church has many organizers, but few agonizers; many who pay, but few who pray; many resters, but few wrestlers; many who are

enterprising, but few who are interceding. People who are not praying are playing.

Two prerequisites of dynamic Christian living are vision and passion. Both of these are generated by prayer. The ministry of preaching is open to a few. The ministry of praying is open to every child of God . . . .

Tithes may build the church, but tears will give it life. That is the difference between the modern church and the early church. Our emphasis is on paying, theirs was on praying. When we have paid, the place is taken. When they had prayed, the place was shaken (Acts 4:31).

In the matter of effective praying, never have so many left so much to so few. Brethren, let us pray.[18]

8

Calling Others to Pray

I am certainly not one of those who need to be prodded. In fact, if anything, I am a prod.[1]

Prodding others to pray is the job of those of us who are already enthusiastic about prayer. We all periodically need a good, swift kick in the area of prayer. The kickers may later become the "kickees," so we need to help one another.

Revivals seem to work in a pattern. A few people are revived. They begin to pray for an awakening on campus, in a church, or in a city. The more they pray, the greater the burden becomes. Since they cannot bear it alone, they need others to bear the burden with them.

So they call others to blend their hearts and prayers with the original few. God then touches these new participants, and they, too, are "set on fire." They then recruit others as well. Thus the numbers who are praying fervently increase.

Sooner or later, a "critical mass" of praying, fervent believers is gathered. As in a nuclear reaction (where molecules of radioactive material are continuously added until a certain mass is reached), eventually an explosion occurs. When a certain number (known only to God) of fervently-praying believers is reached, spiritual explosion occurs. God then sends a sweeping movement to touch the campus, church, or city in order to revive believers and to awaken unbelievers so that they may be converted.

Such a gathering of like-minded souls follows biblical principles of multiplication. We read in Deuteronomy 32:30, "How could one chase a thousand and two put ten thousand to flight unless their Rock had sold them, and the Lord had given them up?" II Timothy 2:2 says, "And the things which you have heard from me in the presence of many witnesses, these entrust to faithful men who will be able to teach others also."

Both verses indicate that more can be accomplished with greater numbers of committed believers. If others are infused with my burden for prayer and awakening, they will, in turn, ignite additional people.

The Seed and the Fire

Dr. Joon Gon Kim of South Korea calls such people "fireseeds," people who bear the seed of the gospel and the fire of the Holy Spirit. They become sparks of revival to set entire nations ablaze wherever they go.

Dr. Kim writes about these fireseeds and what he believes they can accomplish:

> Fireseeds have no limitations. They can glow and grow and burn and blossom wherever they are planted. A fireseed cannot help but grow and multiply if he is equipped with the gospel and the

power of the Holy Spirit. It only takes a fireseed to ignite spiritual fires which in turn set the word aflame.[2]

You may ask, "Has such a fireseed idea worked?" Consider Dr. Kim's results, both in Korea and around the world in the last 25 years:

> The fireseeds in Korea continue to spread in unusual ways. There are fireseeds in the Korean Navy. Presently 100 percent of the Navy ships have Bible study groups. Each begun by one of our fireseeds. Almost without exception every post of the Army has a Spirit-filled man in charge of leading a small group Bible study.

> In the Hyundai Company of Illsan City, 327 Bible studies exist among twenty-one thousand workers. In schools, villages and among professionals we have fireseeds who are responsible to ignite spiritual flames.

> A few days ago one very influential man who became a Christian through our ministry reported to me that, in the Marine College where he holds a position, there are 120 ships, each with a small Bible study group of its own. The ships he ministers on range from small 500-ton ships to 30,000 ton commercial vessels.

> One of our graduate students works for a stock company. This man is the original fireseed for 97 groups from between 5 and 40 people throughout his company. I met his 97 Bible study leaders and found them to be rapidly spreading fireseeds.

> Fireseeds are also spreading overseas. In the Middle East countries our disciples are very active among the 150,000 Koreans employed there. In Thailand, the Philippines, and many other Asian countries our disciples are at work. Our fireseed

disciples are involved in almost every Korean church in the United States.[3]

The Fellowship of the Burning Heart

The gathering of like-minded people to pray is not simply an Asian phenomenon. Rather, this is a pattern which God is using all over the world. One such example occurred in the U.S. in 1947.

Dr. Henrietta Mears of Hollywood Presbyterian Church conducted a collegiate conference at Forest Home in California. One night several committed men joined her for prayer. In the midst of that prayer meeting, God touched all of them in a unique way and produced spiritual awakening in all who were there. One discouraged pastor entered this prayer time late, intending to tell Dr. Mears he was leaving the ministry. Upon joining the group, he, too, was touched by God and found fresh meaning and power in his life. Because they had been touched by God, they wanted others to join them in prayer. From this gathering, the "Fellowship of the Burning Heart" was formed, and its purpose was to call people to join them in prayer and work for spiritual awakening in the world. Among those in this gathering were Bill Bright, Louis Evans, and Richard Halverson. And the results were amazing.

Dr. Bill Bright founded Campus Crusade for Christ. Today its full-time staff number 13,000 in 150 countries around the world. Tens of millions have found Christ through this movement. Dr. Bright says of that experience: "I personally experienced the touch of God at Forest Home in 1947 . . . . I was not seeking the Holy Spirit. But God moved sovereignly, mightily, and powerfully so that my life has never been the same . . . .

I am convinced God [did] . . . more in that sovereign moment than we can do in a lifetime."[4]

Dr. Louis Evans, Jr., later became pastor of the National Presbyterian Church in Washington, D.C. and now ministers to thousands weekly.

The discouraged pastor, Richard Halverson, stayed in the ministry, eventually pastoring the Fourth Presbyterian Church in Washington, D.C. He also was Chaplain of the U. S. Senate, reaching the upper tiers of our government.

Kenneth Scott Latourette, dean of church historians, informs us: "Our reading of Christian history has accustomed us to see God break forth in unexpected places where souls have opened themselves to Him and have been made great by the touch of His Spirit."[5] Calling others to pray for spiritual awakening is one way we can be "made great."

The Momentum Increases

"The history of revivals is the history of prayer movements. Such a movement is now underway in America and around the world, according to prayer leaders at a White House breakfast to mark the National Day of Prayer."[6] Reports like this from a secular newspaper affirm that God is up to something in relation to prayer.

Steve Sellers, National Director of Campus Crusade for Christ's Campus Ministry, recently described going before the Lord for an extended period of concentrated prayer:

Fifty staff from around the country . . . joined us for two days. We had no set program or schedule, [and] there was no personal agenda other than to begin praying, to listen and see where God took us.

Personally, it was unlike anything I have ever been involved in.

. . . The bottom line . . . is that there was a recognition . . . of our need for God . . . . The result is that I feel more serious and single minded [than ever before] to seek God personally and for the Campus Ministry to seek Him . . . . I feel more deeply the need to humble myself before God on an ongoing basis, to ask Him to use me, and to submit myself to whatever direction He leads.[7]

At Ohio University in 1993, J. R. Wurster and other students were instrumental in calling others to pray on their campus. Soon, they formed SPARC (Students Praying for Awakening and Revival on Campus) and called fellow believers on Ohio and Michigan campuses to focus on a fresh move of God. An entire strategy has been enunciated, and hundreds of students have been involved.

Jacques Ellul, French theologian and social critic, challenges terrorists of the world to lay down their arms and give themselves to prayer as the only genuine hope for social change:

Whoever wrestles with God in prayer puts his whole life at stake. In the combat in which man has no reservations, God wills also to have no reservations; and if God has already given everything in His son, then he expects man both to take Him with complete seriousness in prayer and also to conduct himself responsibly . . . .

To engage in prayer is to perform the basic act of a disciple, and at that moment one is radically alone before God . . . . God does not tolerate lukewarmness . . . . As long as we are not engaged in the combat of prayer, our radicalism is necessarily a discourse only . . . ." Apart from prayer, action is necessarily violence and falsehood . . . .

Prayer by contrast is a much more radical break, a more fundamental protest. In that decision, in that combat, the world can have no part, since we have a share in the prayer, that sacrifice, and the resurrection of the One Jesus Christ. Precisely because our technological society is given over entirely to action, the person who retires to his room to pray is a true radical.[8]

A student at Georgia Tech began to pray that God would touch the fraternity system on his campus for Christ. At that time, he was the only one whom I knew who was praying like this, and he really did not know how God would answer. As he prayed, he began to enlist some of his fraternity brothers to pray with him and to work for the evangelization of the fraternity system.

From that prayer group grew a Bible study in his house which eventually increased to 70 men. Other Christians began to hear about this movement and expressed a desire to pray and work for the evangelization of their fraternities, too. At the end of that year, there were over 200 fraternity men involved in Bible studies and outreach—all because one student enlisted others to pray with him.

All over this country, I believe there are students just like you who could allow God to use them to pray and then call others to join with them in prayer. Think of what God said about Joshua as he prayed for a miracle to enable Israel to win a vital battle: "There had never been such a day before, and there has never been another since, when the Lord stopped the sun and the moon—all because of the prayer of one man!" (Joshua 10:14, The Living Bible) If each one of us will be like Joshua, every university in our land could be aflame for Christ.

If you believe you need to open yourself to God and allow Him to bring revival through you, individual prayer is where you start. But you cannot finish there. You also need to call others to join you and share your burden. The more who join you in prayer, the quicker revival will come. As Jack Taylor says, "Prayer gets us in the channel of revivability." The more people who "tune into" this channel, the greater the number of awakened people. And the sooner the awakening will come.

9

Results of Spiritual Awakening on Campus

> The really effective agency of religion in the life of
> the college was the revival . . . which brought so
> many . . . into church and into the ministry. Most
> college presidents and college faculties of this era
> felt that they or God . . . had failed a collegiate
> generation, if once during its four years there did
> not occur a rousing revival.[1]

Can you imagine the president of your college or
university apologizing to the seniors at graduation
because there had been no spiritual awakening on
campus during their collegiate stay? Such might happen
if we met the criteria for our part in laying awakening's
foundation. Only God brings awakening. We cannot
program His work. He has outlined our part in preparing
a way. But when we do our part, a spiritual awakening
could produce some predictable results.

The outworking of revival seems to fall into four areas:

1. Holiness of life for believers.

2. Obedience to God and His Word.

3. Increased power from God.

4. A massive movement of God's Spirit in evangelism.

Notice that these form the acrostic, HOPE (Holiness, Obedience, Power, Evangelism). An examination of each of these areas follows.

Holiness of Life

As Christians enter the channel of revivability through prayer, their moral lives improve. And when revival finally comes, it touches others who have not previously been burdened by the Holy Spirit for personal change.

The Spirit forcefully touches their sin, convincing them of their need to confess, repent, and make restitution. Individuals then lay aside their old habits and unholy lifestyles and walk in fellowship with Christ.

The Asbury College revival of 1970 demonstrates this. We earlier discussed the prayer which led to awakening there. Students began to give testimony to the changes Christ had produced in their lives. Then other students spontaneously began to rise, confess their sins, and ask for forgiveness. All classes were canceled and the chapel service continued unabated for 185 hours (nearly eight days!). Students found themselves ceasing immorality, drugs, drunkenness, cheating, and swearing. They began serious Bible study, evangelism, honest work, and loving their neighbors.

But there was more.

They began to take the message of this revival over the country to Christian schools nationwide. Nearly 40 colleges were either directly or indirectly affected. While covering this unusual "religious" happening, even a major network cameraman was touched. Hearing the confessions and testimonies and seeing the newly-changed lives of students, he put down his camera, walked to the altar of the college chapel, knelt, and gave his life to Jesus Christ. If the secular and the Christian campuses of America were to be awakened today, surely hundreds of such conversions would occur.

Tragically, many believers behave like unbelievers. Because Christ is not Lord of their lives, many Christians participate in many of the same sinful activities as their non-Christian neighbors. As a result, unbelievers "write off" Christ and His power. Never have we needed holiness more!

Among other things, demonstrations of holiness would result in decreases in abortions, an increase in sexual abstinence, and a disinterest in pornography. Other demonstrations of holiness would include the closing of many campus bars as owners see the changed lives if students. Voluntary honor codes might spring forth. Even the tone of campus newspapers might reflect new lifestyles. The fraternity and sorority system would reflect less prejudiced values. In short, students would desire to change instead of being forced to.

Obedience to God and His Word

The second major result of awakening on campus will be the process of obedience to God and His word. Revival is by nature a new submitting of ourselves to God. One of the first steps in preparing for revival is humbling ourselves before Him and beginning to do what He says.

People begin to study, honor, and believe God's Word. It becomes their most valuable text. Instead of ignoring God's promises and commands, they start exercising faith in them.

This new willingness to do what God says also has a great impact on the needs of others. Revivals almost always have clear, long-term effects on social problems. Before revival comes, believers too often care for themselves rather than for the needs of others—particularly if others are invisible to their own social group. But as believers become revived and take the Word of God seriously, they discover many commands dealing with the poor, the hungry, the defenseless, the imprisoned, and the oppressed. In the past, revived believers established hospitals, orphanages, and halfway houses. Dr. James Montgomery Boice comments: "The best things that have ever happened in history have been as a result of that kind of movement, whether the Great Awakenings or the revivals of Wesley and Whitfield."[2]

Revival today could very well produce a new concern for unborn infants and their rights, while maintaining compassion for the parents. It might result in a declining suicide rate and more Christians counseling those who are depressed. A full-scale student movement might be initiated to represent the cause of Christ in the academic world. We could see clear thinking about international politics and war, with open forums for all relevant convictions to be expressed in a responsible and unintimidated manner without fear of "political correctness."

Ethics without legalism could again have a place in the business, medical, and professional schools of our universities. Racism and prejudice, endemic in our society, would be honestly admitted. Wrongs could be confronted.

College students are among the most idealistic groups today. Awakening in the collegiate world could give eternal perspective to that idealism and generate new solutions of ancient problems both here and abroad.

Increased Power from God

The Holy Spirit is the only One who brings revival to people and locations. He is the power source for all that occurs. I Corinthians 4:20 says, "For the kingdom of God does not consist in words, but in power." When the Holy Spirit infuses our lives, Jesus said, "you shall receive power . . . ." (Acts 1:8)

Because awakening causes believers to be more obedient, the Spirit can release greater power. To Robert Wilder, leader of the Student Volunteer Movement (which itself came out of the revival of the mid-1800's), Rev. A. J. Gordon said: "God is ready to give you the power of His Spirit as soon as you are ready to obey Him."[3]

This power means the power to pray. It means power to forgive. It means power to love. It is power to have courage in the face of fear. This power will enable believers to stand firm and fight graciously and humbly (if necessary). Most of all, it will be power to "go the distance" in the Lord's ministry.

An excellent example of this is the Student Volunteer Movement. From its founding in 1888 until 1928, it is estimated that 20,000 students went as long-term foreign missionaries. This was the greatest student missions movement in history. Many of these missionaries stayed on the field for 20-30 years. They remained committed for life. Such is the result of the Holy Spirit's long-term power.

Great Movement of Evangelism

Revival never comes without producing a sweeping movement of evangelism. Consider again the Welsh revival of 1905. In the space of three months, 100,000 were converted, and 80,000 of these were still in churches five years later. Winning people to Christ became the activity of every revived church member—not just that of a select few.

Evangelism was a focus of revival in the 1800's as well. In 1854, Dr. W. S. Tyler of Amherst College made a survey of recent awakenings in 11 Northeastern colleges. He found that 34% of the students on those campuses had become Christians and nearly half of those converted were studying to become ministers. He asked for prayer for more awakenings and pleaded: "Why, we ask again, should not every year witness a revival in colleges, and every class . . . receive a fresh anointing from on high? . . . Why should any individual leave unconverted?"[4]

How about our campuses today? We have mentioned revivals in the 1700's, the 1800's, and in the 1900's, when as many as three-fourths of the student body of various universities like Yale, Princeton, and Cornell were converted. But some of these things also are starting to happen today.

In a secular university in Alabama, several thousand students (nearly 10% of the student body) are trained every week in evangelism and in discipleship and are reaching every person on that campus every year for Jesus Christ.

At Miami University (Ohio) one recent year, Christian students shared their faith with virtually every student on campus.

At the University of Texas, two prayer meetings lasting several hours each drew 350-400 students. These were the largest such meetings recorded there in recent years.

When revival comes, thrusts such as these become the norm, not the exception. It occurs not only because the believers are revived in their holiness, obedience, and power, but also it occurs because the unbelievers are more deeply convicted of their sin and need for Christ. Such great numbers of unbelievers desire to come to Christ that believers are compelled to tell them how. Dr. J. Edwin Orr observed: "In times of revival we believers must work like doctors in an epidemic." But rather than catching a disease, it is an epidemic of people catching a cure!

Dr. J. Sidlow Baxter, who pastored in Edinburgh during a time of great spiritual awakening, was once asked by a friend of mine what it was like when revival came to his church. He replied: "I can only say that anywhere and everywhere you went God was in the atmosphere. People talked of no one but God; people thought of no one but God. People went to work as usual, but God was the focus of all their attention."

"God . . . in the atmosphere." This may summarize what it would be like if awakening comes to our campuses. That expectation alone seems worthy of the vast amount of prayer, humbling, and confessing that must precede it.

There is much more that could be said about the results of revival. Actually, God may surprise us all. He is the God of the unexpected and does far more than we could ever hope or ask or think. But one thing we can know for sure—when He does come, no one will be able to miss it. His movement is going to be powerful, it is going to be sweeping, and it is going to be significant for virtually every student, administrator, and faculty member on campus.

Make a list of what you and your cohorts believe God could do on your campus when revival comes. Include names and places as God brings them to mind. Your list might include things like the dean of students becoming a witnessing Christian, a particular dormitory having 500 or more in Bible studies every week, a certain person stopping his drunkenness or immorality, etc.

Dream big. Then begin to ask God to act upon the things on your list and to expand your vision to believe Him for even greater things. Expect your campus to explode in spiritual awakening soon.

10

Conclusions

> It is my sincere prayer that the burden which God
> has given me for spiritual awakening in our day
> may be the heart-cry for revival.[1]

I believe that revival on campus is not only needed, but
also revival is essential. I also believe that it is coming.
If it does not come, I see very little hope that the darkness
on the colleges and universities of our country will be
lifted at any time in the foreseeable future. If there is
no revival, many will still be won to Christ and many
will be discipled. But I do not see any way that the
current influence of unbelief can be reduced apart from
the sweeping movement of the Spirit of God.

But revival is coming. I think there is a tidal wave of
dissatisfaction growing among Christian students today
concerning the spiritual apathy that exists. There is a
disgust with campus prejudice against Christ and His
followers. But there is also a growing movement of
prayer for revival and meeting God's prerequisites for it.
Examples from past and and current events indicate that
the Spirit of God is doing something highly significant,

perhaps something that has not happened since the last great student awakening in America in 1905.

The movement of people creating the environment for revival is swelling. Each of us needs to be a part of this movement and not miss what God is doing. Our tendency is to become trapped in our own apathy, materialism, and "the-way-we've-done-it-for-years" thinking. But the time for business as usual is over. It is now time for some new beginnings. And committed and obedient believers can be a part of what God is already bringing to pass.

In 1983, 20,000 university students gathered in Kansas City for a conference called KC '83. They learned how to become fireseeds and how to bring spiritual awakening to their campuses. It was one of the two largest gatherings of Christian college students in America's history.

Yet awakening did not come when they returned to their campuses. Initially, there was widespread enthusiasm for prayer and for laying the foundation for revival. But after about a year, it became more difficult to maintain as other interests intervened. Seniors graduated, and freshmen entered. The new students had no experience of fervent prayer and were less interested in praying for revival than their predecessors. The movement faltered.

In the last few years, though, zeal has begun to be restored. Increasing numbers of prayer movements are springing up. Students are understanding anew the long-term necessity of prayer, confession, and calling others to do the same.

It seems that students on our campuses are beginning to grasp that we are in a battle for the minds and souls of men and women. The stakes are not simply temporal, but eternal. The destiny of the world is involved, not simply our own comfort. The greatest hope of our globe is revived university students who are still unfettered by mortgages, mediocrity, or man-made distractions—students who will relentlessly serve Christ. Imagine men and women on campuses calling the universities of our country to allow Jesus Christ back on the campus, to allow Him to be Lord of all.

If we fail to heed the rallying cry of our great Captain Jesus Christ, then the enemy of our souls may come in like a flood, and we will find ourselves trapped by our own inaction and uncaring attitudes. Worse than that, we will have dragged hundreds of thousands of others down with us into the morass of our own indifference.

This book's purpose is to challenge you from indifference to becoming an insurgent for spiritual awakening who will pray and believe God to do something sweeping on your campus. If you do, I believe your life will be significant beyond anything you could have ever hoped in terms of making a difference—not only in our country, but also in countries around the world.

If you are not willing to become a fireseed, you will probably be ensnared by the sea of mediocrity in which most college students find themselves. You could well come to the end of life asking: "What did I accomplish of significance or eternal value? I wonder if I fulfilled my purpose in life?"

Let me invite you to become one of those revolutionaries who is praying, working, and expecting the Lord to revive believers on campus and awaken unbelievers to the glory of His name.

During the massing of German forces on the coast of France for an invasion of Great Britain in World War II, Winston Churchill made a speech that called on his countrymen to stave off disaster. His call on a temporal level is the same call I would like to give you on a spiritual level. Try to hear in these words the voice of God speaking to you about your part in the revival to come:

> What General Weygand called the Battle of France is over. I expect that the Battle of Britain is about to begin. Upon this battle depends the survival of Christian civilization. Upon it depends our own British life and the long continuity of our institutions and our empire. The whole fury and might of the enemy must very soon be turned on us. Hitler knows that he will have to break us in this island or lose the war. If we can stand up to him, all Europe may be free and the life of the world may move forward into broad sunlit uplands. But if we fail, then the whole world, including the United States, including all that we have known and cared for, will sink into the abyss of a new dark age made more sinister, and perhaps more protracted, by the lights of perverted science. Let us therefore brace ourselves to our duties, and so bear ourselves that, if the British Empire and its Commonwealth last for a thousand years, men will still say, "This was their finest hour."[2]

May this be your finest hour!

NOTES

Preface

1. Charles Malik, *The Two Tasks* (Westchester, IL: Cornerstone Books, 1980), p. 26.

Chapter 1: Let's Turn the College Campus Rightside Up

1. *The American Freshman: National Norms for Fall, 1992,* December 1992, p. 2.
2. *Atlanta Constitution,* June 9, 1994.
3. J. I. Packer, *A Quest for Godliness* (Wheaton, IL: Crossway Books, 1990), p. 36.
4. Quoted in *How to Make Your Mark* (San Bernardino, CA: Campus Crusade for Christ, 1983), p. 19.
5. *Ibid.*
6. Charles Finney, *Revival Lectures* (Westwood, NJ: Fleming H. Revell, n.d.), p. 33.

Chapter 2: Awakened at Sixteen; Awakener at Twenty-Six

1. Earnest Baker, *The Revivals of the Bible* (Cape Town: T. Mashew Miller, 1986), p. 83.
2. Timothy C. Wallstrom, *The Creation of a Student Movement to Evangelize the World* (Pasadena, CA: William Carey International University Press, 1980), pp. 24-25.
3. J. Edwin Orr, *Campus Aflame* (Glendale, CA: Regal Books, 1971), p. 27.
4. *Ibid.,* p. 101.

Chapter 3: Five Prerequisites for Revival

1. Alexander Solzhenitsyn, "A World Split Apart," *National Review*, July 7, 1978, p. 836.

2. Quoted by Stephen F. Olford, *Lord, Open the Heavens* (Wheaton, IL: Harold Shaw, 1980), p. 92.

3. *Atlanta Constitution,* November 28, 1987.

4. *Wall Street Journal,* December 10, 1993.

5. *The Oregonian,* May 5, 1993.

6. *The Atlanta Constitution,* February 2, 1983.

7. *San Bernardino* [CA] *Sun,* July 7, 1992.

8. *USA Today,* February 9, 1994.

9. *USA Today,* March 3, 1989.

Chapter 4: Humility and Its Role in Revival

1. Richard J. Foster, *Prayer—Finding the Heart's True Home* (New York: HarperCollins Publishers, 1992), pp. 60-61.

2. John Pollock, *Billy Graham: The Authorized Biography* (Grand Rapids, MI: Zondervan Publishing House, 1966), p. 52.

3. *Wall Street Journal,* February 7, 1994.

4. "The Church Search," *Time,* April 5, 1993, p. 49.

Chapter 5: Confession and Repentance

1. Richard Owen Roberts, *The Solemn Assembly* (Atlanta: The Home Mission Board of the Southern Baptist Convention, 1989), p. 8.

2. J. Oswald Sanders, *Prayer Power Unlimited* (Chicago: Moody Press, 1977), pp. 147-148.

3. M. Scott Peck, *The Road Less Travelled* (New York: Simon and Schuster, Inc., 1978), pp. 32-33.

4. "Eights Days That Shook Asbury," *Worldwide Challenge,* March 1983, p. 19.

5. J. Edwin Orr, *Campus Aflame* (Glendale, CA: Regal Books, 1971), p. 231.

6. Stephen F. Olford, *Lord, Open the Heavens* (Wheaton, IL: Harold Shaw, 1980), p. 86.

Chapter 6: The Supreme Example of Prayer

1. S. D. Gordon, *Quiet Talks on Prayer* (Westwood, NJ: Fleming H. Revell, 1967), p. 11.

2. Quoted by Stephen F. Olford, *Lord, Open the Heavens* (Wheaton, IL: Harold Shaw, 1980), pp. 62-63.

3. J. Oswald Sanders, *Prayer Power Unlimited* (Chicago: Moody Press, 1977), pp. 28-29.

Chapter 7: The Power of Fervent Prayer

1. William R. Bright, "The Great Adventure," *Worldwide Challenge,* May-June 1994, p. 45.

2. *Atlanta Constitution,* November 14, 1988.

3. Charles Finney, *Revival Lectures* (Westwood, NJ: Fleming H. Revell, n.d.), pp. 72-73.

4. *Ibid.,* p. 137.

5. Quoted by Manny Hooper, *Worldwide Awakening and Revivals, 1700 Onwards* (Pasadena, CA: Research Center for Revival and Missions, 1989), pp. 6-7.

6. Kenneth Woodward, "Talking to God," *Newsweek,* June 6, 1992, p. 40.

7. "God Goes Back to College," *Newsweek on Campus,* November 1986, p. 10.

8. "Excerpts From a Recent Brown University Prayer Meeting," *Newsweek on Campus,* November 1986, p. 10.

9. Eldon Johnson, "The Covenant Alliance of Prayer Newsletter," Unpublished Issue of December 1993, p. 5.

10. Earl and Trish Pickard, Newsletter, September 25, 1991.

11. Bob Caswell, "What He Has to Say About Prayer," *FrontLines,* Spring 1984, p. 4.

12. Auburn University Campus Crusade for Christ Newsletter, February 16, 1984.

13. David Bryant, Letter to Author, 1982.

14. "Counting Every Soul on Earth," *Time,* May 3, 1982, p. 67.

15. J. Oswald Sanders, *Prayer Power Unlimited* (Chicago: Moody Press, 1977), p. 154.

16. Dr. Joon Gon Kim, "It Only Takes a Fireseed," U. S. Campus Ministry Director's Letter, Campus Crusade for Christ, April 27, 1982.

17. Dr. William R. Bright, "The Holy Spirit and Revival," Letter to Campus Crusade for Christ Headquarters Staff, Spring 1993.

18. Leonard Ravenhill, "No Wonder God Wonders," Great Commission Prayer League.

Chapter 8:   Calling Others to Pray

1. Winston Churchill, *Churchill, The Life Triumphant* (New York: American Heritage Publishing Co., Inc., 1965), p. 94.

2. Dr. Joon Gon Kim, "It Only Takes a Fireseed," U. S. Campus Ministry Director's Letter, Campus Crusade for Christ, April 27, 1982.

3. *Ibid.*

4. Dr. William R. Bright, "The Holy Spirit and Revival," Letter to Campus Crusade for Christ Headquarters Staff, Spring 1993.

114

5. Quoted by J. Edwin Orr, *Campus Aflame* (Glendale, CA: Regal Books, 1971), p. 202.

6. *Atlanta Constitution,* May 9, 1992.

7. Steve Sellers, National Campus Ministry Director's Newsletter, Campus Crusade for Christ, April 2, 1993.

8. Quoted in *Discipleship Journal,* 1984, pp. 31-33.

Chapter 9: Results of Spiritual Awakening on Campus

1. Frederick Rudolph, Quoted by J. Edwin Orr, *Campus Aflame* (Glendale, CA: Regal Books, 1971), p. 226.

2. "Interview with James Montgomery Boice," *Discipleship Journal,* 1982, p. 43.

3. Quoted by Timothy C. Wallstrom, *The Creation of a Student Movement to Evangelize the World* (Pasadena, CA: William Carey International University Press, 1980), p. 35.

4. W. S. Tyler, *Prayer for Colleges* (New York: M.W. Dodd, 1855), pp. 142-143.

Chapter 10: Conclusion

1. Stephen F. Olford, *Lord, Open the Heavens* (Wheaton, IL: Harold Shaw, 1980), p. 11.

2. Winston Churchill, *Churchill, The Life Triumphant* (New York: American Heritage Publishing Co., Inc., 1965), p. 91.

Additional copies of this book may be ordered by calling:

1-800-729-4351

(Visa, Master Card and Discover Accepted)

or writing to:

Campus Crusade Direct
4307 East Third Street
Bloomington, IN 47401
Fax (812) 339-8389

Campus Crusade Direct is a distributor of Campus Crusade for Christ materials for use in evangelism and discipleship. Please call for information about available resources.